Roots *to*
Radiance

NIKITA UPADHYAY

Roots *to* Radiance

Wholesome Beauty Solutions for the Millennial Life

EBURY
PRESS

An imprint of Penguin Random House

EBURY PRESS

USA | Canada | UK | Ireland | Australia
New Zealand | India | South Africa | China | Singapore

Ebury Press is part of the Penguin Random House group of companies
whose addresses can be found at global.penguinrandomhouse.com

Published by Penguin Random House India Pvt. Ltd
4th Floor, Capital Tower 1, MG Road,
Gurugram 122 002, Haryana, India

Penguin
Random House
India

First published in Ebury Press by Penguin Random House India 2019

ISBN 9780143447566

Typeset in Sabon by Manipal Digital Systems, Manipal

Printed at Manipal Technologies Limited, India

www.penguin.co.in

For my family and loved ones

Contents

Part II Tips and Hacks

Foreword

Beauty is as beauty does. Time and again, we've been using this phrase—but it's time we give it some serious thought and adopt it in our lives. I strongly feel that while some people have great symmetry, skin and looks, what eventually makes them gorgeous and radiant is the vibe, thoughts and actions they have to match their looks.

As clichéd as it may sound, there are a million reasons to imbibe healthy and positive thoughts and vibes into your lifestyle . . . The health of your skin has a direct link to the thoughts you hold in your mind and heart. Whatever the struggles you might be coping with—anxiety, insecurity etc.,—having good thoughts is where you should start from if you wish to achieve a healthy, truly beautiful skin.

The idea of beauty has evolved greatly in the recent years. It has found support in the growing sense of sisterhood among women and the understanding that beauty is not about perfection. For me, true beauty lies in the grace of trying to achieve a goal while acknowledging what has already been achieved so far. Along with embracing and celebrating your imperfections, beauty also lies in cultivating your own personality and having an in-depth understanding of what works for you—as opposed to blindly following a general, stereotypical notion of it. Beauty is too vast an idea and means different things to different people.

The fact that ageism is being called out, the fact that wrinkles are being celebrated, the fact that all shapes and sizes are being loved and respected, is an obvious proof of how healthy and easy it is for imperfections to coexist while you are in the process of transforming yourself.

Wanting to defy ageing and preventing premature wrinkles is not anti-self-love—not appreciating how far you've come in the development process is! Striking that perfect balance where you are working towards looking a certain way while being comfortable with how you currently are is the right approach to finding real 'beauty' and being beautiful.

But there's a flip side to such acceptance as well. As great as acceptance might be, an unhealthy lifestyle and letting yourself go mindlessly is an abuse/misinterpretation of freedom. While letting your hair down once in a while is the right approach, habits like constantly having junk food or being a couch potato are not to be encouraged.

We live in the age of social media where various activists, many of them self-proclaimed, are altering our physicality—whether it is the texture and colour of our skin, or the shape and size of our bodies. I think these are the things that we should start analysing and questioning. It's critical for us to celebrate authenticity and honesty and truth, because I think if you perceive beauty from a prism that does not come from an authentic, true source, it is a hindrance in the mission of celebrating the greatness of how it has evolved.

Becoming conscious of yourself after looking at a picture of a 'perfect' girl that appeared on your Instagram feed versus taking an honest opinion from reliable people in your life to tell you what is best is a no-brainer. For me, constructive criticism comes from my mother and the women who work for me. Whether it's my manager, my personal assistant or my stylist, these are women who empower me every day through their jobs. They are my reality checks—the most honest people in my life who tell me things as they are. I always get an absolutely unfiltered response on any question I ask them. And in many ways, I think they form my voice of reason . . . Because it is unjust to give the power of shaping *you* or making you insecure to that girl on social media who made you feel so instead of to the people who know you best.

Does that dress really complement your body type? Is a certain shade of lipstick the best pick for you? If you can't decide that on your own, remember, that 'perfect' girl in those TV ads or Instagram feed shouldn't be deciding it for you either. It's the people who notice, interact and deal with you on a daily basis that you can allow to shape you . . . The relationships that strengthen you are the relationships that matter, and it's their opinion you should consider if at all.

My husband is one of my biggest sources of love, affection and security—and my friends are my storehouse of the support and courage I need at every stage of life. Our beauty and glow is an outcome of how much we're loved and cared about. While your husband/father/brother/son's attention gives you one kind of security, the women in your life secure you differently . . . Trust sisterhood! I'm the only child and I know how far depending strongly on your friendships can take you as you get older.

When you are younger, your DNA takes care of the changes and transitions you go through. As you grow older, it becomes harder to maintain gorgeous skin without a more disciplined lifestyle. When I was in my mid-twenties, I was fairly aware of how my hormones were going to play a big part in my skin health. But it was only when I crossed my late twenties that I started recognizing other essential aspects and methods that effectively contributed to the benefit of my skin. When you are younger, you don't really think about using sunblock or jump into make-up and run out and do your work. But as time passes and the lines start appearing on your face, you have to figure out your best-suited regime and make regular time for it.

That's the thing you learn as you grow older—you realize the difference between quality and quantity. Over time, your friend circle might grow smaller, but it gets richer in terms of quality—you figure out the people who are capable of nourishing your soul.

Same is the case with skincare. It's only after hoarding a whole bunch of next available 'new improved' products that you are able to narrow it down to a few quality ingredients that do you good. True beauty is hardly achieved without going through a journey.

But the current times are not solely about acquisition. The way you contribute to the beauty industry makes a huge impact too! The way you make your purchases and get your skincare and make-up in order shapes the whole circuit of beauty.

The transformation capabilities of organic products are insane. It's amazing how certain ingredients can take away all your problems. It's crazy how you don't even have to step out of your house to banish most of your skin concerns. It's surprising how incorporating some organic and wellness routines can help you live a longer, healthier life. Being a holistic beauty advocate and doing environmental-friendly campaigns all my life, I can tell you there's no bigger power in the world than that of nature. It goes beyond planting more trees, protecting nature and using these totally economical, yet supremely powerful, organic methods . . .

But here's the paradoxical part—when brands claim to be all-natural but package heavily in plastic, they're still contributing in harming the environment. And when you affect the environment poorly, you're actually affecting your own health.

Through this book, I would like to reach out to people and ask them to influence their friends and family to do their bit and make the most of nature's offerings. One must start realizing the benefits of holistic beauty that not only empowers our own idea of beauty but also strengthens our community. By strengthening communities, I mean most natural products are made by women and children at the grass-roots level . . . when you put your money into what these communities create, you validate the relevance of what they do by securing that community financially. They feel secure and don't fear going out of business.

When I was titled Miss Asia–Pacific, I was just nineteen and, apart from the obvious and predictable plans I may have had to get it, my mission was to communicate effectively. Which, years later, I'm still doing.

The way actors have to be responsible for the roles they play and the image they portray to the public, every single individual should take ownership of what we're putting out there. I recently shot a campaign where the women in the story were doing a deeply entrenched gender-stereotypical role. I insisted that we get the man to do these things as well so that we reflect a home that upholds equality. I believe that if we try to make the content we put out not so stereotypical, we'll be surprised to see how these refreshing flips can change mindsets. Making the world more diverse and warm can do volumes for self-confidence.

Talking about diversity, there's a powerful shift on the diversity front. We've finally established that every woman is beautiful irrespective of race, caste, colour and everything beyond. That whole unfair narrative is totally changing now—I feel that's very positive. All of this stems from working towards a more equal space for people of all colours and all strata of society. It's all about the desire and the drive to make the world a better place.

I believe all these acts of fairness are interconnected and make a difference.

I cannot count how many girls I know who have developed eating disorders and disturbed their hormones due to stereotypes and trends imposed on them by social media. I see little girls being obsessed with selfies or posing keeping their hands on their hips and I feel this behaviour is worth questioning. A lot of damage to mental health is being done by these online platforms that could be very easily used to communicate effectively and bring change. Not every girl has to work towards bringing a change, but one definitely has to think about the repercussions of what they represent.

Like most things, beauty too is a two-way street . . . meaning, you'll have to match your inside to the outside. Apart from basic things such as finding the right moisturizer and lotions, internal nourishment also plays a very critical role. Exercise plays a significant part in skin health, but the most powerful tool to balance and maintain good health is mental balance. Striking that balance is where you start if you want to end up achieving true radiance on the outside and peace on the inside. That's the richest form of self-love.

Self-love isn't about obsessing over yourself or looking down upon people for whatever imperfections they may have. That's what most people get wrong about it. Self-love and empowerment is to feel fabulous in your current state while making women around you feel the same way about themselves. The idea that a woman is woman's worst enemy is now being proven wrong, more than ever.

I myself have always been extremely effusive and forthcoming in celebrating the achievements of my colleagues, especially women. In any industry, especially ours, women are constantly pitted against each other, where you're constantly compared for your looks, roles, personal lives, you name it . . . women are making it a point to fight back. If you speak to any of the leading ladies in the film industry today, you'll recognize how forthcoming they are in their praise for their colleagues and how supportive they are of each other and that's very important. This may not have a direct link to the idea of beauty, but this is about women uplifting women and making women around you feel safe, secure and full of joy. It's about creating a healthy, non-toxic environment where females can cultivate positive thoughts and shine their way to inner and outer beauty.

When I had my first conversation with Nikita about this book's foreword, her vision seemed to resonate with me in a very surprising way. It was as if she was covering all the points I strongly care about. Whether it's holistic beauty, empowerment, environment and beyond, as we delved deeper into different aspects, I realized that she has such a fresh take on things we must explore through this book. Even something as basic as how nature's components work and applying that phenomenon to simplifying your life is explained with an interesting twist. Given her insightful articles on health and wellness on social media and websites, I think she has cracked the code to being the millennial voice we need. The approach taken to address skin concerns, relatable struggles, and going through them while holding your head high is the kind of approach I want the younger segments to learn from. This is not just a reference bible for all things beauty—use this book to feel good about yourself, to laugh off the difficult bits of life that may seem impossible, and to match the progress of your outside with your gorgeous inside.

Apart from the 500+ tips and tricks from her, the beauty experts who've stepped in to contribute for the book ensure how well she's got you covered for this mission of achieving your #SkinGoals.

* * *

My Beauty Dos and Don'ts

When it comes to maintaining a disciplined beauty routine, don't underestimate the power of not having an aggravated nervous system. Regular exercise, meditation and yoga are stressed on for a reason. When I say exercise, I mean even running and regular exercises make you release endorphins . . . it just releases the right hormones to enhance skin quality and physical health.

The understanding that skin is the biggest and foremost reflection of health is important. Health is a result of mind and body . . . and body of course is connected to nourishment and exercise.

One of the things that I do that has positive effects on skin health is meditation. It's a big part of my daily discipline. Every day, as soon as I wake up, I don't touch my phone for the first 20 minutes. I make sure I meditate after I've had a glass of water and 5 almonds.

That's my pure protein intake as soon as I wake up.

I meditate for about 20 minutes after that, and only then do I get on with my day's work.

Before I sleep, I make sure I centre myself. I do a full body scan and some exercise. Whether it's yoga or functional training—exercise is a crucial part of my lifestyle.

I follow a 90 per cent vegetarian diet. I eat a lot of raw fruits and vegetables. I maintain a highly nutritional food intake in general. I get my dose of proteins from almonds, quinoa, and I do eat plenty of leafy vegetables. Staying well hydrated and drinking lots of water is the oldest rule in the book, and guess what, it never fails you.

My usual routine involves drinking something I'd like to call 'yellow tea', which is basically warm water with turmeric, ginger juice and honey, before bed. It is extremely beneficial for our body and it also aids the immune system.

As far as using green beauty products is concerned, I don't use any moisturizers, cleansers or skincare products that have any chemicals.

The products I use are all natural water- or oil-based.

I definitely scrub my face once a week.

I'll let you in on this easy DIY scrub that I use. The contents are powdered apricot and walnut mixed with either rose water or aloe vera extract to scrub off impurities and dead skin.

For people with dry skin like mine, a deep-moisturization skin mask is crucial. I use under-eye masks and face serums regularly. I make sure I wear sunblock every day. It goes without saying that I never go to bed with make-up on—that's rule #1. That cleansing process before sleeping is essential.

But here are a few things that I don't do. I don't go for clean-ups and facials; I don't use soap on my face—I've never used those harsh chemicals ever. To top it off, I cultivate healthy thoughts. Mental health can't be neglected.

—Dia Mirza,
13 March 2019, Mumbai

Introduction

My parents are not the ones to impose a whole lot of rules. Nine years ago, when I was moving out, I knew I was free to choose the kind of lifestyle I wanted for myself.

Moving from a small town in the state of Chhattisgarh to Delhi, I was aware and cautiously hopeful that life was going to change for me in matters of significance as well as of insignificance alike, needless to state, in more ways than I could reckon. Little did I know that even if I was going to major in fashion design, I'll eventually end up going back to doing what I enjoyed doing the most in high school—writing.

From the cosy comfort of waking up to three kinds of fresh pressed juices next to the bed to having no one wake me up at all, this was the time I was set to let the intelligence of life take the wheel and to offer me the scary yet wonderful chance at reinventing my life.

Another usual shift of the changing hues of the sky, and suddenly, here I was, totally answerable for the result of me—far away from the usual faces, yet naively vulnerable to the new. It's a delicate thing—freedom! The food I ate, the thoughts I processed, the life pattern I followed—every damn thing would come to define me in a way like never before. Little things making a significant impact and things of importance deciding which way the current flows. I knew that living by myself, and using public transport in a city quite infamous for pollution wasn't going to be easy.

When you look good (not that I don't)—all praise and blame to a mother who looks twenty-five at fifty—and you find yourself alone and stupid in a city not exactly celebrated for being nice and respectful to women, the capital of a country that boasts of a cultural legacy quite celebrated for worshipping the feminine, it can get seriously confusing and tough. All said, looking good is crucial, and thanks to the shift in urban consciousness, men would agree too. My homework was done well, I was sure of that—introducing Ayurvedic and organic methods into life that make you more confident and evoke a sense of discipline in your conduct.

There's a strange kind of empowerment that comes to you when you take complete charge of your concerns and banish the bad for good.

'We do not inherit the earth from our ancestors; we borrow it from our children.' This American proverb may have its roots in the quite neglected fact that we take our planet for granted, quite unapologetically so. Not to forget how the only creatures with developed minds to walk on the planet seem not only determined to neglect the offerings of mother earth, but also ignore its cries for help in the process.

When I compare my hometown to any metropolitan city, I can name a dozen things that, back there, I do not have access to. However, it's not such a bad thing. Necessity being the mother of invention, people in smaller towns have much healthier alternatives to our so-called daily need products up their sleeves. And that's what I've been meaning to share in this book. That's the purpose of this. To arm millennials like myself with healthy choices and alternatives to looking good, amidst all the cacophony and constant streaming of hundreds of products claiming to be the go-to-it for our daily wardrobe issues of surviving, even emerging victorious, with ease in a world overripe with an untiring unforgiving economic engine, and doing it all while looking good.

If there's one thing millennials are known for, it is for our knack to hack our way to getting what we want in life.

And time and again, we've been told that there are no shortcuts. But what most people fail to notice (or perceive) is that we also look for a cause and meaning to everything. And we do give the due patience to things we believe in. And all the skyrocketing success of anti-animal cruelty, women empowerment, veganism and organic fashion is a proof of that.

Centuries before cosmetics and chemicals took over, the Egyptians used clay and olive oil paste as soaps, milk and honey as moisturizers, even body sugaring for hair removal, and the Chinese were busy restoring their youthful skin with jade rollers (that are back in trend, btw!).

But, even after all this evolution, it's mesmerizing how we still like to know if there's a historical backing to a newly launched product. Is it vegan? Does it have ancient herbal ingredients? Is it all natural (like it claims to be)? The questions are endless but the concern is just one. If it's natural, it's harmless, hence no harm giving it a shot.

Why rely on chemicals in the first place when we Indians have more than just 'use coconut oil to soften your cuticles' as a tip from the ancient beauty book. In fact, you'll be humbled to find out how the rural areas of our country are practising a rare set of ways to bypass skin concerns that are a goldmine of DIY hacks.

Belonging to a small town has not only given me primary exposure to the lesser-known skincare secrets (that eventually contribute to fitness and wellness), but it has also taught me the importance of getting back to basics. To love make-up—but to love real skincare a million times more.

I am blessed to have a parent who has fed and treated me with those secrets before I moved out to live in a big city. I was prepped by parents who wanted to make me immune to the mental and physical challenges that were coming my way.

My book, *Roots to Radiance*, has been written with an objective to bring back the power of organic living into our routine. From superficial beauty to wellness, nature has solutions to multiple problems that we experience every day.

For me, my mother, who is in her fifties but looks like she's twenty, is living proof of what a DIY, organic lifestyle can do. And this book is to record as much as I can in one place to be able to refer and suggest to my mates out there.

Mom and me

But before I get to that, I want to ask you all one question: What's the best self-love or self-care advice someone has given you?

If you ask me, I'd go with a piece of advice my mom gave me. She asked me to be my own mother to assess every situation. Whether it's reviewing my lifestyle and eating habits or trying to achieve those unrealistic body/beauty standards social media teaches us to live up to.

'Love, nurture, care, rebuke and supervise yourself—like I would,' she says.

And from my experience, I can tell you that applying this one rule has brought so much discipline and confidence in my conscience.

Because shielding yourself with natural goodness is what your biggest well-wisher would want for you.

Mother Earth, Mother Nature, our Magna Mater is capable of so much healing.

From plants and herbs that can erase the existence of a number of diseases and concerns, it also has the power to shield your well-being just as a mother would.

And if you can't do that, here's another interesting parenting tip I learnt from Kate Middleton and Prince William via Internet obviously—Do you notice how they always crouch down to talk to their kids? That technique is called 'active listening', meaning when you're making a physical effort to talk to your child, you're boosting their self-esteem and letting them know they're important. Now this advise is not from my mother, it's from me! If you can't mother yourself, treat yourself like you're your own precious child. Aim at lifting you mentally. Doing so will unlock a whole new level of self-love, self-care, self-worth for you. Beauty walks hand in hand with high thinking.

So gear up to enter the world of appreciating nature's offerings, going high on gratitude, and always remember—holding your head high is not situational, it's a way of life.

Or as my friend Matthew Higgins, a self-made millionaire would say: Don't compromise your integrity even when you're drowning. Just hold your head high to stay above the water and you'll be fine!

Bobbi Brown's Letter to Millennials

When I got in touch with Nikita in the early 2019 and she told me she was writing this book and wanted my input, I asked what it was going to be about, and she said, 'In your chapter, I want you to inspire women in beauty.' After a thorough discussion of how we should go about it, we decided it would not be a chapter about beauty tips. It will be about life lessons and believing in yourself. As I've always said, the more positive you are, and the more confident you are, the more gorgeous it makes you look. Beauty is about goodness from within, and yes, tons of confidence.

While we were discussing more about the book, my plan of coming to India was on the cards, but wasn't certain. I certainly didn't know that a dinner with her over candid conversations was just sixty days away; it's crazy how small the world is. We got on video calls to discuss what this book was about, and how culturally rich and beautiful I thought India was. In my years of studying women, no matter where they came from—different countries, races and cultures—the most appealing thing about them was their zeal and what drives them.

We decided this would be a motivational letter to women who were in as well as outside of the beauty industry. While 'typical' beauty lessons are included throughout this book, I took the opportunity to use this chapter to feed your soul with positivity, through my personal life lessons.

As a make-up artist I have worked with women from many different countries. What is inspiring to me is realizing that we are all very different—our skin colours, our lip colours, our eyelid colours. I used to study the colour of the lips of models, my kids' babysitters, etc. I was fascinated by the different skin tones. I realized there was no make-up in the market to enhance the natural skin tones of people, and that led me to designing my own make-up line. The idea was not to change the shade or colour of their features; it was about celebrating everyone for who they were. True beauty is always in the details, and oftentimes, the unique characteristics of a person's face.

Teenage girls can be very overwhelmed by the sheer number of choices available to them. Millennials are stressed, not only because of how competitive the world has become, but also because of the many options making it difficult for them to get a clear picture of who they are. I myself went to three colleges until one day it became crystal-clear to me what my path was. What you want to do should fascinate and speak to you.

Since I was a young girl, I loved make-up and I loved playing with it. I liked how pretty I felt when I had it on, and I also loved watching my mom do her make-up. I didn't know that I would enter it as a career. My mother asked me, 'If it's your birthday and you could do anything you want, what would you do?' I said, 'I would love to go to the department store and play with make-up.' She said, 'Why don't you study that in college?' So that is what I did. It was my third and last college. They let me design my own major, as they didn't have make-up as one, but they allowed me to get a fine arts degree with a focus on theatrical make-up, and that's what I did. And I pretty much designed my own programme, which led me to being an entrepreneur. So, *long story short*—that's the thing about wishes. If you wish for just one thing, it'll lead you straight to the arms of your true desires. Life's too short not to give that a shot.

You don't have to know everything in the beginning. Baby steps are simple. Take them! When I was younger, I didn't even think about being an entrepreneur—I was just thinking about how I was going to pay my rent. I waitressed, and I moved to New York to volunteer doing make-up for magazines. It was a slow process, it didn't happen quickly, and I never thought about having my own line. One day, I thought of making a lipstick that was different from what was already available in the market. I made it and thought my friends, models, editors might buy this, but I never thought it would be a company. The first big editorial piece on the line was for one of the biggest beauty magazines, and I could not believe how many I sold after that. Trust your journey.

Not having the resources to put a plan in place is not the worst situation. I never understood what the term 'brand' actually stood for even when I was starting out. My company evolved when people started hearing about me. I was still working as a make-up artist at the time, while also making cosmetics. I was being written about in magazines and getting on morning shows to talk about beauty and make-up once a month. People really started to know who I was. Even when my brand and I were becoming popular, my struggles didn't end. I'll never forget this one order where the cases kept falling off the lipsticks so we had to delay the launch and get the top of those lipsticks to fit. I was firefighting the packaging struggles, doing TV shows, doing make-up, etc., without having a clear picture of where I was headed. It was okay for it to be unclear, as long as I was heading somewhere.

When I first started, the market was about a more artificial look. I had to work very hard to explain to women how much better it looked when they just enhanced their natural skin tones to get a sun-kissed, flawless, radiant look. In just four years, we got a phone call from the biggest beauty brand in the world making an offer to buy our brand.

I had finally convinced an artificial make-up-loving market to flaunt their natural selves instead. I did not fit in, but I had started a revolution. There were times when I had to do everything from scratch, and times where we had people to help me with everything. I went from being a small company to becoming a part of the major leagues and having the infrastructure and staff to do everything I wanted. There was plenty of transition when my company sold, but what remained constant were the amazing creative directors, copywriters and staff I had. They constantly said I was an inspiration to them, but really, they were inspiring me. You will see women bringing each other down, but you can also see women holding each other's hands to achieve their goals.

Your vision is your win. I've had many people weigh in their inputs to influence the formulae, the marketing and the philosophy of my brands from time to time, and those campaigns didn't do nearly as good as they would've if they went by my vision. You are the truth! You must be bold. You have the right to announce what's right and take the actions you take. Trust that instinct.

In my sixties now, I've launched a new wellness brand, my own podcast, come out with my ninth book, a lifestyle website and a boutique hotel.

When Nikita asked me if I have ever wished to retire, I said I can't imagine myself not working. I try so hard to shut my brain off but it is really difficult. I let it make noise, and listen to it.

When the time came, after 22 years of serving as the CCO at my namesake brand, I had to move on, and let go of my name, without knowing what's on the other side. My ninth book is about beauty on the inside out, and that led me to create my wellness brand. It was my art and inclination that showed me the next step. As I've said, there are all kinds of days—some amazing, some horrible—and when hard times strike you, you have to know that the solution is in you. It's in your capabilities, and the key to the way out is probably sitting right in front of you.

Not everyone is going to join hands with you on your ideas. When you stick to what you believe in, hold on to it tightly, and show them how it's done. I've had people mock my ideas, and do the same thing five years later when it becomes a trend. I'll let you in on another personal story from many, many years ago when digital insanity was about to pick up. I was invited to an Eastern European country to speak to the editors of a major publication. Their magazine had just started to have financial troubles, so they asked me, 'What would you do?' I said, 'Honestly, I don't understand when we're reading an editorial and I see an outfit, why can't I press the button and get the outfit.' They said, 'Nooo, this will never happen.'

Well, guess what's happening now? Being ahead is a gift given to a chosen few.

Trust is your weapon. Instinct is your path. And self-belief looks good on you!

—Bobbi Brown
17 March 2019, The Bahamas

Part I The Body

1

Face

The index of your mind, heart and soul. Our imperfections are not half the reflection of how much we're taking in. Managing life, work and mess . . . it's time for a #Shoutout to how terrific we are anyway!

Fellas, let's *face* it . . . there's a reason why this is Chapter 1.

When you're in hurry (which is basically every morning), it all comes down to perfecting your face over anything else.

Waking up early, attempting to follow the ideal morning rituals, making breakfast, getting ready and then kicking some serious butt at work . . . and still not feeling like enough was done . . . How much does a girl have to do? Whenever I feel overburdened with #LifeStruggles, it takes me back to that scene from *Sex and the City* S1E11 where Samantha tells Carrie, 'Men don't want to know women are human.' Meaning they're expected to be perfect all the time.

But I'd say, forget men, going by the amount of judgement there is out there, everyone has shown us how nasty it can get, not to forget our own judgements.

Imperfections are beautiful . . . but we all know how crazy it gets when you are after a pimple or a blemish to go away, when it's seem to have moved and settled down permanently on your face, without paying rent.

I'm sure you've had one of those days when you spent one hour to get ready and no one (relevant) saw you, but when you dressed down, made a messy bun and went out, everyone you knew was in that supermarket.

A *Forbes* article even said that casual dressing can keep you from getting a promotion![1]

And as much as I would like to permit you to do what you like, and be the way you want to be, life will teach you that putting your best foot forward each day, looking your best beautiful every moment, and moving forward with fierceness is the only way to be.

On that note, let's establish some basic morning rules:

As dermats say, it's always better to switch products from time to time than using the same products throughout the year. This chapter will provide you the knowledge of what your skin needs round the clock—how to start

---

[1] Victor Lipman, 'How Your Clothes Can Help You Get Promoted', 8 June 2018, https://www.forbes.com/sites/victorlipman/2018/06/08/how-your-clothes-can-help-you-get-promoted/#629b9c817e47

and end the day and how to prep your skin according to the season.

As they say, the first step to looking good is feeling good. And morning being the index of the day . . . should be started right! While you're double-tapping every meme on social media that encourages you to snooze your alarm, be a couch potato and finish a full pizza on your own, you must know that you can unlock the best version of you only when you're disciplined.

Starting your day right isn't as difficult as it sounds. Just a few ground rules adding to your morning routine can take major beauty concerns off your chart.

Something as small as the way you wash your face impacts how you'll look years from now. Surprising, isn't it? You'll be more surprised about what I'm about to tell you—you've been washing your face wrong, all this time!

What most people think is that in this busy and hurried lifestyle, how does it matter how you wash your face as far as you lather it up, and wipe it clean? Except it does! And most of us tend to move our fingertips in downward circular motions, causing your skin to sag over time. Most of us are also guilty of keeping the water temperature too high and applying excess pressure on the skin. And this is how you make it right:

Wash your face by making your fingertips go in upward circular motion, and when you splash lukewarm water on it, make sure you do that in upward motion too. While wiping your face with a tissue or a towel, make sure you don't wipe your skin totally dry. It's always better to leave your face a little wet to make your moisturizer application more even. Moisturizer blends better when the natural moisture of your face eases the application. Doing so keeps wrinkles and sagging skin at bay for a long, long time. To keep your skin tight, remember not to stretch your face in downward motion while washing the nose and cheek or brows area. The rule is to bring your fingertips together and massage it in upward motion to make your features more pointy.

This is a habit my mother made me incorporate quite early in the day.

In other words:

- Use lukewarm water for rinsing.
- Wash your face with a suitable cleanser in upward motion.
- Massage your face in a way that it doesn't expand the surface or apply too much pressure. Don't completely wipe your face dry before you apply moisturizer.
- After you're done moisturizing your face, this 60-second facial exercise is the therapy your skin needs. The point between your eyebrows, aka the third eye point, has the power to grant so many gifts to your body and add to the productivity of your day in ways you can't imagine. Place your thumb in between your brows and gently hold it upwards for a minute. This trick helps you reduce muscle tension and improve brain functions. It'll also unlock the energy centre that's present under

the surface of your skin, causing it to promote better circulation. The self-massage acupressure technique not only has a rejuvenating effect on your body, but prevents wrinkles, sagging skin and negative metabolism.

- That's a five-minute plan to having a beautiful day right there.

How to End the Day?

Well, when you have a start that is so easy-peasy, you owe yourself a plethora of options to choose how to end your day. Whether to brighten, smoothen, depigment, or clear your face, each day you can pick a concern to fix to eventually get the skin of your dreams. This chapter will make you dive into the sea of natural ways to clear, unclog, de-tan, or whatever it is that you want to do. Although I intend to spoil you with more DIY options for your body, it's necessary to tell you that you can use all of these masks and scrubs for your body as well.

1. Fruit Juice for Your Face

Madhuca longfolia, also known as mahua, is a small green-coloured oval-shaped fruit. Extracting the juice of this fruit and applying it to your face at night will help you achieve a stunning glow over time. Ages ago, our ancestors used to extract the juice of its seed to use as a soap too!

2. Skin Toning and Tightening

Asian skin doesn't have to care about wrinkles for a long time. But, as they say, the smart ones start early. Brands bringing in 'Anti-Ageing before Ageing' products only hints that the needs of the masses involve starting early.

The ideal age to start anti-ageing and collagen-boosting products for Indian skin would be 25. In this chapter, I will be addressing all possible skin concerns with some mind-blowing organic hacks that'll not only help you fight your skin issues, but also prepare you for what's to come.

Starting with skin toning, here are some skin-tightening masks that'll make-up for your skin's collagen cravings and also save you from spending a bomb on salon treatments.

MASK 1

¼ cup rose water
¼ cup cucumber juice
½ cup black lentil powder (*urad* dal)
¼ cup carrot juice

- Mix the rose water, cucumber juice, black lentil powder and carrot juice in a bowl. Create a thick paste.
- Apply and leave on for 25 minutes.
- Rinse and apply moisturizer.

Doing this twice a week will help you prevent sagging skin.

If you have dry skin, I suggest you add *malai* (cream) to the ingredients for added smoothness.

If you have oily skin, stick to the basic ingredients of this recipe.

MASK 2

¼ cup water
¼ cup ground oatmeal
2 tablespoon chickpea flour (*besan*)
2 teaspoons honey
2 tablespoons curd
1 egg white

Oatmeal powder and besan are ingredients that bind when mixed with water. Hence they have tightening capabilities. Honey and curd tone the skin and make it smooth.

- Boil ¼ cup water and add the oatmeal powder and *besan* to make a thick paste. Make sure you're not using instant oatmeal.
- Add honey, curd and egg white to the paste and apply to the face for 20–25 minutes and rinse.
- Apply your favourite hydrating moisturizer or face serum after using face masks—make it a basic rule.

DIY powder compact recipe

While we're discussing oatmeal, it reminds me of how oatmeal makes for a great face compact for Indian skin tones.

- Grind ½ cup oatmeal and mix with a cup of water to wash the powder.
- Pour the mixture on a sheet of paper and filter the impurities. Once filtered, let the damp oatmeal solution dry.
- When it's fully dried, you can use a brush to apply that powder to your face.
- If it combines and dries as small blocks of oatmeal, grind the oatmeal once again to make a fine powder out of it.

MASK 3

Little less than ½ cup kaolin clay (*chini mitti*)
4 teaspoons raw milk
2 teaspoons primrose oil
2 teaspoons rose water (add if the paste is too thick)

Clays play an important part in the world of face masking. Apart from tightening, different clays have several abilities to exfoliate, nourish, cleanse and smoothen. But there's one standard rule that should be applied before using clay-based masks—apply a thick layer of face moisturizer or cream before the mask.

In this case, primrose is an important ingredient as it tightens the skin. Its omega-6 fatty acids help balance hormonal levels, firm the skin and reduce wrinkles and fine lines.

- Add raw milk, primrose oil and rose water to kaolin clay and make a paste.
- Apply to face after applying face cream and leave the mask on for 20–25 minutes.
- Wash, followed by more moisturizing.

3. Pigmentation Mask

Concealers and under-eye colour correctors are #bae when you have panda eyes. But the burning desire to look amazing effortlessly has led us to find solutions from natural ingredients, which frankly will offer more long-term, healthy fixes.

Pigmentation and dark spots can happen anywhere, but under-eyes, corners of the nose and edges of lips are their favourite locations.

It's almost impossible to find a person who doesn't have pigmentation on some part of their body. It's the easiest to get, considering stress levels, lifestyle choices, insomnia and, biggest of all, pollution! There's a never-ending list of bank-breaking creams that haven't worked on us, we can all agree to that. Here are some DIY, natural recipes to help you depigment your skin while you're on that mission.

MASK 1

½ cup strained *chironji* (*Buchanania lanzan*)
¾ cup full cream milk (raw)
2 teaspoons honey
¼ teaspoon saffron
1 nutmeg

The trick is to make the texture of chironji scrub your face, so make sure you don't crush and strain it too finely. Saffron and nutmeg help fade acne scars and dark spots. Nutmeg powder is also available in the market but I suggest you grind it on your own as it is much more effective.

- Soak saffron in raw milk overnight.
- Grind nutmeg on a coarse platform and keep adding few drops of water during grinding.
- Mix strained chironji, ground nutmeg and honey with raw, full cream milk (that you soaked saffron in) to create a paste.
- Apply to face and leave on for 30 minutes.

Doing so twice a week will help reduce pigmentation.

Note: If you have super dry skin, replace chironji with walnut, use full cream milk and follow the same procedure.

MASK 2

1 washed potato raw, peeled, grated
1 cucumber, peeled and grated
Curd (just enough to massage the problem areas)

- In case of dark circles, apply potato and cucumber juice (extracted from grated potatoes and cucumbers) on your eyes. Potato juice contains a natural bleaching agent that'll help even your skin tone.
- In case of pigmentation, pair the above-mentioned extracts with curd and massage the areas that need to be treated. Feel free to apply this to your full face if you wish to.
- Extract the juice of the grated potato and mix it with cucumber juice and curd and apply to your full face.

Unlike most face masks, this one is good to be applied closer to your eye area—it will help treat dark circles around the eyes, on its way to treating dark spots on your face.

MASK 3

½ cup water
1 black tea bag (or leaves)
A few drops of liquorice extract (easily available online
and one of the most effective oils to help fade dark spots)
A few drops of rosehip oil
2 tablespoons of bentonite clay

If web articles are to be believed, rosehip oil is actually a
big part of Kate Middleton's beauty regime. Three kids
later, the Duchess of Cambridge sure knows how to look
a million bucks each time she steps out.

So, taking a leaf from her book, I've decided to
include this depigmenting oil and add it with another
major pigmentation-fighting ingredient—black tea!

- Boil ½ cup water and dip the black tea bag
  in it.
- When the solution cools off, add bentonite clay,
  liquorice extract and a few drops of rosehip oil.
- Mix it well and make a paste.
- Apply to moisturized face and rinse after
  25 minutes.
- Re-apply moisturizer post masking as well.

4. Smoothening Masks (for all skin types)

We love using primers to create that smooth base
before applying foundation on our faces every morning,
but what if I told you that you can have smooth and

supple skin naturally that'll not only make you subtract applying one chemical-based product from your hectic mornings but also make you feel great about your skin even when you're wearing no make-up at all! Gear up for this organic mask that compliments all skin types, repairs dull skin and eventually gets your #NoMakeUpSelfie(s) to thank you!

MASK 1

7–8 pieces of peeled, sliced papaya
Juice of 1 lemon
2 teaspoons honey
1 teaspoons sandalwood powder

- Grind the papaya pieces to a paste.
- Mix lemon juice, honey, sandalwood powder and apply to your face for 25–30 minutes.

The presence of potassium in papaya, when combined with honey and lemon, makes for an ideal combination to take dullness off your face. Sandalwood powder is a cooling agent that's been added to soothe your skin.

MASK 2

1 banana
2 tablespoons honey
½ sliced avocado
Few drops of grapeseed oil

This is such a fruity mask! All the ingredients in this moisturize and hydrate your face without making it greasy. As cosmetics are majorly dehydrating for the skin, using this hours before putting on make-up can also help your foundation sit well on your face and last longer. The fruits used in this mask are basically internal moisturizers used for external use. Grapeseed oil is like a natural astringent that'll block excess sebum and is totally suitable for people who have oily skin.

- Cut up the banana and avocado and mash them. You can even grind the avocado to make a finer paste.
- Mix honey and few drops of grapeseed oil to the mashed fruits and apply to face and neck. *You can switch grapeseed oil with any oil you find suitable too.*
- Rinse after 20–25 minutes and apply serum or moisturizer if you still feel the need for it. This pack is pretty hydrating on its own, anyway.

MASK 3

4–5 blocks of grated pumpkin or ½ cup pumpkin puree
1 teaspoon apple cider vinegar
2 teaspoon honey
2 teaspoon curd
Pumpkin is packed with anti-ageing properties. With its retinoic acid, antioxidants, beta-carotene and vitamins,

this humble fruit, despite being so cheap, has ingredients found in expensive night serums and creams.

- Add curd to the pumpkin puree and mix well.
- Then add apple cider vinegar and honey to the paste and apply to face and neck.
- Keep it on for 20 minutes and wash.

Face Smoothening Oil

1 teaspoon extra virgin coconut oil
A pinch of turmeric

This mask is the Duchess of Sussex's favourite. Meghan Markle's facialist Nichola Joss has recommended this inexpensive blemish-clearing face mask that'll make you radiate after you apply it to your face. Just mix the two ingredients and apply it to your face, 20–25 minutes before your face wash or pre-sleep shower. Do not use more than the recommended quantity of turmeric and in case it made your skin too yellowish, just add a few drop of lemon juice to raw milk and dip a cotton pad in it. Wipe your face gently with the milk-soaked cotton pad.

If you have dull and dry skin, this will work like magic.

Turmeric will even your complexion and coconut oil will moisturize your face to give it a dewy look.

How to make coconut oil at home

Since there are many recipes that involve coconut oil in this as well as the following chapters, here's the easiest way to make multi-purpose coconut oil at home:

2 coconuts (brown ones that have water in it)

¼ cup water

Two coconuts are enough to make an adequate amount of coconut oil at home.

- Smash the coconuts and pour the water in a glass.
- Remove the hard shells and blend the coconuts in a mixer. Then add some water and coconut water to it.
- Make sure you've blended it as fine as you can and then strain all the extract/water out of it and store in a glass jar.
- Refrigerate the jar overnight. The next morning, you'll find a thin layer of coconut cream on top of the surface of frozen coconut water.
- Remove that layer of coconut cream and heat the water in medium heat on a saucepan.

Your coconut oil is ready. You can use it for cooking, for your skin, hair—*anything*!

5. Acne-Fighting Masks

YES, we're finally here. The basic millennial life problem. Pimples!

Acne, adult acne, cystic acne, pimples, acne scars, zits—there's so much to this. It is plain annoying how these guys enter our lives quite early, in our teenage days, and take forever to leave. And from trying every rule in the book to epically failing and carrying evidence of #ExperimentsGoneWrong on our faces, we try our best to make the stay of these bad boys as tough as possible.

Bad hygiene, dirty pillowcases, oily scalp, pollution, dust, hormonal imbalance—everything results in acne. It's like it is impossible not to have one. And you know—it's okay. If you haven't popped a pimple, hoping it to vanish overnight (and then waking up with a bigger pimple the next morning), have you even lived life?

On a more serious note, don't pop that pimple. It only makes it worse. Instead, slowly and steadily win this race. Develop more sincere habits and establish a routine to manage the issue.

Here are some DIY recipes of natural ways to control acne:

MASK 1

1 cup water
10 basil leaves
5 neem leaves
2 tablespoons Fuller's Earth (*Multani Mitti*)

A few drops of eucalyptus oil
A few drops of lavender oil

Eucalyptus dries acne, and basil and neem have anti-inflammatory properties. Lavender brings in some more soothing, and Fuller's earth absorbs excess oil and eliminates impurities from the skin, and even from hair.

- Strain and boil the leaves in a cup of water.
- When the water cools down, filter out the leaves and add the clay and oils.
- Apply the mask to the face and keep it on for not more than 20 minutes and rinse.
- Use a water-based serum or non-oily cream post masking.

MASK 2

½ cup aloe vera extract
2 teaspoons lemon juice
A few drops of tea tree oil
Pulp of 2–3 pieces of oranges
This mask is a citrus blast on your face. Since your skin craves Vitamin C when it breaks out, this is an easy and effective mask to apply on regularly.

- Mix aloe and orange extracts with lemon juice and tea tree oil and create a natural gel mask.
- Apply to face and keep on for half an hour.
- Wash and apply best-suited cream.

MASK 3

½ cup water
3 large betel leaves (*paan*)
petals of 1 rose (*desi gulab*)
1 tablespoon chickpea flour (*besan*)
2 cotton seeds
A few drops of moringa oil

Betel is a cooling agent and cotton has absorbing capabilities. Moringa oil is ideal for people with oily skin and chickpea flour binds the whole formula.

- Tear up the betel leaves and boil them in half a cup of water and keep it aside to cool.
- Crush and mix desi gulab petals with cotton seeds fine enough to add to a paste.
- Mix the chickpea flour and the betel water and the paste (above) and add rose petals to it.
- Mix well and add few drops of moringa oil and apply to face for about 20–25 minutes.

6. DIY Masks for Dry Skin

Oily skin may be problematic, but when in control it can actually be considered the best skin. Acne-producing excess sebum is proof that your system is capable of generating excess oil. But the reverse happens once one starts ageing and skin starts to get more and more dry and the problem is worse when you've always had dry skin.

Dry skin needs more treatment and attention as ageing starts to show on dry skin earlier than on oily skin.

With proper love and care, dry skin too shall pass all the hurdles that keeps it from being smooth and radiant.

Here are a few DIY masks for dry skin:

MASK 1

2 teaspoons muskmelon seed (*kharbuja*)
2 walnuts
½ cup raw milk
1 pinch turmeric
Turmeric and raw milk boost glow, and muskmelon improves blood circulation and is rich is potassium and Vitamin A, among other things.

- Add the pinch of turmeric in raw milk and soak walnuts and muskmelon seeds in it.
- Once the two are well-soaked, grind them with the turmeric milk and apply to face for 25–30 minutes for a radiant glow.
- Repeat twice or thrice a week.

MASK 2

4 almonds
½ cup water
A few drops of almond oil
3 teaspoons cream
2 teaspoons pumpkin seeds

- Soak almonds in a cup of water and peel them.
- Crush the almonds and pumpkin seeds and add almond oil.
- Apply paste to face and leave on for 20–35 minutes before rinsing.
- Follow your regular moisturizing routine post masking.

MASK 3

1 tablespoon wheat bran (*chokar*)
½ cup milk
1 Vitamin E capsule
Chia seeds

Wheat bran's depigmenting properties and richness in antioxidants makes it bag a spot in this recipe. Chia seeds, with their fatty acids, help smoothen the skin, make it look livelier and shoo away dullness. Vitamin E helps you get your glow game on, and milk—well there is a reason why Cleopatra bathed in it.

- Soak chia seeds in milk for a few hours.
- Add wheat bran flour to that milk in a bowl.
- Cut open a Vitamin E capsule and pour its extracts into the bowl.
- Mix all the ingredients well and apply to your face to get an instant glow.

Repeat twice or thrice, as per your requirement.

If you're on a busy schedule, just take a small amount of cow ghee in your fingers and apply to your face every day. This will take away all your dry skin concerns. It will hydrate, nourish and smoothen your skin in NO time!

7. Reversing Sun Damage

Social media may trick you to believing in #InstaQuotes that say, 'Quit your job, travel, get a tan, never come back.' But in reality, you do care about your job, as you do for your skin. And when that has been sunburnt after a vacay, you will be asked, 'What the heck happened?!!!'

The following tricks are not just masks, but also exciting ways to reverse the damages from sun exposure in the *coolest* ways possible, literally.

MASK 1

¼ cup watermelon juice
¼ cup cucumber juice
¼ cup lemon juice
¼ cup potato juice
3 teaspoons sandalwood powder
A few drops of peppermint oil
A few drops of rose water

- Mix the juices with sandalwood powder and add a few drops of peppermint oil. Apply to your face for instant cooling effect.

This mask is ideal for people who get sunburnt easily and get redness due to sun exposure.

Alternate method

- Mix rose water, watermelon juice, cucumber juice, lemon juice, peppermint oil and fresh potato juice with the sandalwood powder.
- Pour the solution in an ice tray and put it in the freezer.
- After a few hours, when the solution is frozen, rub these cubes on your face gently after sun exposure.

The calming and soothing properties of the above ingredients will work as an after-sun protectant for your skin and help you reverse the post-sun-exposure damage that keeps bothering your skin even after you return indoors.

But if you think that's not enough, here's how you can make an after-sun mask with almost the same ingredients.

MASK 2

¼ cup watermelon juice
¼ cup cucumber juice
1 teaspoon sandalwood powder
1 teaspoon multani mitti

- Mix and make a paste out of these ingredients and store in your fridge.
- Keep applying post sun exposure to get rid of sunburn and make your skin happy.

MASK 3

¼ cup carrot juice
¼ cup tomato juice
3–4 teaspoons red lentil powder
Aloe vera extract
A few drops of rose oil

Tomato juice alone is a great natural sunscreen. Carrot juice nourishes the skin, helps fix skin disorders and fights redness. Red lentil powder helps remove tan, and rose oil and aloe extracts soothe and even skin tone.

- Grind enough red lentils in your grinder and store it to keep reusing.
- In a bowl, mix together the aloe vera extract, tomato juice and carrot juice.
- Add a few teaspoons of the lentil powder to the mix.
- When the mixture is ready, add rose oil and mix well before applying to face.
- Repeat twice or thrice in a week, depending on sun exposure/damage.

MASK 4

2 sliced strawberries
½ cup raw milk
7–8 mint leaves
2 teaspoon rice flour

Strawberries fight tan and act as a great face scrub and anti-ageing agent too. Rice flour is anti-inflammatory and has ferulic acid and allantoin, which are sun protection components. Mint refreshes your face and milk treats discolouration.

- Grind sliced strawberries and mint leaves with raw milk.
- Add rice flour and make a paste.
- Apply to face to de-tan and rejuvenate.
- Repeat twice or thrice a week, depending on sun exposure/damage.

8. Remedies to Shrink Open Pores

Nothing ruins your make-up faster than open pores. I'm saying it because I've experienced it first-hand. Open pores let the skin breathe, but there's more to it. Every pore has a hair follicle in it and it secretes oil, hence the excess sebum.

Do you ever do your make-up and feel like your face looks ashy after a few hours? And it get's worse when you already have oily skin that constantly makes you take breaks to powder your nose. It's because you have open pores that are secreting oils, making your face look greasy.

Pores, big or small, should be neutralized by home remedies such as those that I'm going to talk about in this section. Here are a few recipes to help you shrink open pores with ease.

MASK 1

1 ice cube
Lemon juice
½ sliced banana
1 tablespoon honey

- Wash your face with lukewarm water to open your pores and then apply ice to shrink them.
- Mash the slices of banana and add lemon juice and honey to create a paste.
- Apply it to face to shrink open pores over time.
- Use this mask every alternate day to enjoy the smoothest skin ever.

MASK 2

1 egg white
1 teaspoon chickpea flour
A few drops of lemon juice
A few drops of pomegranate oil
A few drops of clary sage oil

Pomegranate oil fights bacteria in clogged pores, and clary sage oil helps shrink the pores. Lemon, chickpea flour and egg whites shrink your pores in the process of benefiting your skin in other ways, like tightening your skin.

- Crack the egg and separate the white.
- Add chickpea flour, lemon juice, pomegranate oil and clary sage oil.
- Apply a thin layer on your face and wash after 20–30 minutes.
- Repeat twice or thrice a week.

MASK 3

1 kiwi
3 tablespoons unflavoured yogurt
A few drops of lemon juice
Kiwi is packed with Vitamin C and is amazing for the skin.

- Grind kiwi and mix it with yogurt and lime juice to make a paste.
- Apply to face and keep on for half an hour.
- Rinse and moisturize.
- Repeat twice or thrice a week to manage open pores.

9. Face Scrubs

We've come to the 'most skipped' part of our beauty regime. I asked ten girls I knew about their beauty regime, and even though they're quite into skincare and all, they did not mention exfoliating as a part of their routine.

In order to make your make-up set evenly on your face and, not to mention, remove dirt, excess oil and impurities, scrubs should ideally be a very important part of your routine. Exfoliating at least twice a week will help you achieve your skin goals faster. Massaging gently in circular and upward motions, these DIY natural scrubs can be used for face, neck and body. Although I will talk about body and lip scrubs separately, let's get you to exfoliate your face first.

MASK 1

¼ cup rose water
2 teaspoons coconut oil
1 tablespoon white sugar
Sugar is a fabulous for scrubbing and for your face and scalp too.

- Mix rose water, coconut oil and sugar and exfoliate your face using circular, upward motions (as explained earlier), twice or thrice a week.

MASK 2

2–3 figs
½ cup raw milk
1 teaspoon almond oil
1 used green tea bag

Previously, in some recipes, I talked about Cleopatra's famous milk bathing fact. In this recipe, I'm including—what was said to be her favourite fruit—fig!

Fig has micro-granule-like particles in it and is capable of doing wonders for the skin. This fruit is not only a great exfoliator but is also capable of neutralizing free radicals and playing the role of a natural antioxidant.

- Soak figs in raw milk until they become soggy.
- Grind the figs and add green tea leaves and almond oil to make a paste. Tiny particles in fig and small green tea leaves will exfoliate your face and green tea leaves even correct the effects of pollution on the face.
- Use this scrub twice or thrice a week. Apply a moisturizer after.

Use this scrub as a mask, adding occasional drops of water and massaging in circular motion, right before washing as another way to use this mask-in-scrub.

MASK 3

1 tablespoon curd/buttermilk/unflavoured yogurt
2 teaspoons oatmeal powder/gram flour
1 ½ tablespoon honey
½ peeled pomegranate
½ tomato or juice of one tomato

This mask will clear your complexion, fix open pores, remove tanning, as well as scrub your face.

- Grind the pomegranate seeds and tomato for just a few seconds to make a paste. Make sure you don't grind it too fine as you need the paste to be grainy to be able to scrub your face.
- Add curd/buttermilk/unflavoured yogurt, honey and oatmeal powder/gram flour.
- Mix all ingredients well and apply to face and gently massage in circular motion for 15–20 minutes.
- Rinse and apply serum.
- Repeat twice or thrice a week.

10. Make-Up Removers

If you're one of these people who just wash their faces to remove their make-up—STOP!

Your face wash alone can never take off a day's worth of make-up, dust, impurities, excess oil, etc. You need a make-up remover that hydrates your face in the process of taking your make-up off. Excessively dehydrating cosmetics can steal away moisture from your skin. In this chapter, I've formulated some make-up removers that you can make using your favourite essentials, and they'll also be gentle and loving to your skin, just like you deserve it.

a. Aloe–Lavender Make-Up Remover

3 tablespoons aloe vera gel
3 tablespoons apple cider vinegar
2 teaspoons olive oil
A few drops of lavender oil

Olive oil alone can make for a fab make-up remover, but using these ingredients together makes a perfect balance of natural scents, astringents and soothing gel to make sure you take your day's make-up off in the most nurturing way.

- Mix the aloe vera gel, apple cider vinegar, olive oil and lavender oil together.
- Take a cotton pad and use this formula to take off your make-up.

b. Eucalyptus–Rosemary Make-Up Remover

½ cup water
2 teaspoons liquid castile soap
2 tablespoons rosemary oil
A few drops of eucalyptus oil

The way the previous recipe had apple cider vinegar as a natural astringent, this one has rosemary that plays the same role. Eucalyptus oil has anti-inflammatory, antibacterial properties to help you cleanse off your make-up without leaving behind the chemical residues of your dehydrating make-up products.

- Mix water with the liquid castile soap and oils, and wash face accordingly.

c. Bergamot–Lemon Make-Up Remover

½ cup water
2 teaspoons baby shampoo or liquid castile soap
1 teaspoon coconut oil
2 tablespoons lemon oil
A few drops of mandarin oil
A few drops of bergamot oil

- Mix water with baby shampoo and add the oils and mix thoroughly.
- Use a cotton pad and this formula to remove make-up with a citrusy twist.

Antibacterial Make-Up Brush Spray

30 ml distilled water
6 drops of tea tree oil

A few years ago, news about an Australian model went viral, showing her swollen face that was a result of using dirty, unwashed make-up brushes. Not that we needed that as a reminder to wash our make-up brushes regularly, because, hello? Basic hygiene! But, for a lazy girl who loves make-up, that news will really give you a scare as well as plenty of motivation to keep them clean.

So introducing a two-ingredient spray that'll not only keep your make-up brushes free of fungus but will also prevent you from getting pigmentation and acne.

- Mix distilled water with a few drops of tea tree oil, and store it in a spray bottle.
- Spray this solution on your washed brushes after they've dried. You can keep spraying it even after you've used the brush to apply foundations, blushes, concealer, etc.

Tea tree oil can be used to treat fungal infections on skin as it kills blemish- and acne-causing bacteria in a jiffy.

11. Face Washes

If you ask me, I have two face washes because I don't think my face needs the same amount of deep cleansing each time I wash my face. So, I have one tea tree foaming wash that I use after I'm done removing my make-up with a cleansing balm and micellar water, and the other one that is a pH-neutral face wash for the times I just need a soft cleanse. And it's of the good experiments I've done for my skin.

But nothing beats the face washes my mother used to make with different ingredients. From trying different ingredients to bake a cake to making these custom shampoos and soaps, I've seen it all as a child. Here are some face wash recipes that will take off your daily grime and balance your skin.

a. Honey–Lemon Face Wash

1 cup water
½ cup castile soap (liquid)
2 tablespoons honey
2 teaspoons almond oil
1 tablespoon eucalyptus oil
5 teaspoons of lemon oil

This face wash is great for people with acne-prone skin.

- Mix liquid castile soap with water and add honey.
- Then add all the oils and mix thoroughly.
- Pour it in a bottle and use the solution as a face wash.

b. Aloe–Lavender Face Wash

½ cup distilled water
½ cup liquid castile soap
2 teaspoons aloe vera gel
2 teaspoons jojoba oil
2 teaspoons glycerine
7–8 drops of lavender oil

This is a soothing face wash for all skin types.

- Mix castile soap with water and add aloe vera gel, glycerine and oils.
- Mix well and pour into a bottle you can store this face wash in.

c. Mint–Charcoal Face Wash

½ cup liquid castile soap
¼ cup multani mitti
¼ cup olive oil
3 tablespoon peppermint oil
1 full teaspoon activated charcoal
1 teaspoon chia seeds
1 teaspoon rosehip oil

This is a scrub face wash, ideal for skin with open pores.

- Mix castile soap with olive and peppermint oil and mix thoroughly in one bowl.

- In a separate bowl, add the multani mitti, chia seeds and activated charcoal. Mix it thoroughly.
- Then mix both of these mixtures together in little proportions till it's all fully blended and devoid of any chunks.
- Then add rosehip oil and mix everything well once again.
- Store this in a pot or a bottle. Use lesser proportions if you think you can't finish it as fast because we're not using any preservatives.

12. Face Serums

If you have combination skin, serums are great. Not because they don't make serums for oily and dry skin, but because water-based serums complement and balance combination skin in a way like no other. In this particular chapter, where there's an elaborate set of recipes to treat every facial concern, face serums are pretty basic yet very effective.

Finishing the course with the right serum is the key to unlocking your best beautiful.

Here are a few facial serums that you can apply pre and post make-up removal. Serums work great when applied overnight. So gear up to have happy mornings if you apply these DIY natural serums the night before.

SERUM 1

¼ cup glycerine
¼ cup rose water
A few drops of almond oil
A few drops of lemon juice

This is a great night serum especially for winters.

- Mix these ingredients in a glass bottle and keep the bottle exposed to indirect sunlight for a week.
- Start applying the mixture to your face every night before going to bed.

You may increase the quantity of the ingredients when making this serum, to be applied every day for a month or so.

SERUM 2

1 teaspoon moringa oil
A dash of sandalwood oil
Aloe vera extract

These are all cooling agents. Moringa oil mattifies the face and is ideal for those with oily skin.

- Mix these ingredients and apply to the face before sleeping to soothe the skin overnight and wake up more gorgeous.

SERUM 3

1 teaspoon castor oil
1 teaspoon almond oil
1 teaspoon coconut oil
½ cup rose water

This is for those of you who have dull and dry skin.

- Mix castor, almond, coconut oils with rose water and shake well.
- Apply to face after your last face wash of the day.

SERUM 4

Aloe extract
Vitamin E capsule

- Cut open a Vitamin E capsule and mix it with aloe extract and apply to your face before sleeping.
- This will feel thick on your skin, so make sure you've mixed the capsule content well with the aloe vera extract. You can blend this with aloe vera gel as well.

13. Face Mists

Face mists are just a great way to freshen up your face in the middle of a workday or on the go. In this section, I will help you customize your own face mist with the scent and essential oils of your liking. The whole thing about scents and memories is so personal. They're able to evoke your senses like nothing else.

For me, lavender is one essential oil that I like to experiment with. I like to mix it with face masks, oils, serums, foam washes—everything. Lavender has soothing properties and can be used in multiple ways.

So of course a mist that has lavender can help treat anxiety and also freshen my face (and mood) on a hard day.

The recipes of this chapter will train you to do exactly that. You can pick a pair of compatible oils and come up with a way to keep your skin hydrated in a fun manner with these mists. And what's better? You can totally use them as body mists!

a. Green Tea Toner Mist

¼ cup cucumber juice
¼ cup aloe vera extract
10 petals of desi gulab
½ cup green tea water

- Mix the green tea water with the aloe and cucumber extracts and add the desi gulab petals. Shake and mix well.
- Pour it in a spritz bottle and use as a detoxifying toner.

b. Calendula Lavender Soothing Mist

10–15 calendula flowers
1 small cup water
5 teaspoons lavender oil

- Steep the calendula flowers in hot water and then filter them out. Let the water cool down.

- Then add lavender oil and stir well.
- Pour it in a spritz bottle as use as a soothing toner.

This is amazing for those who develop redness and rashes easily.

c. Rose Jasmine Night Toner

1 cup water
7–8 jasmine flowers
3 teaspoons rose oil

- Soak the jasmine flowers in a cup of water overnight.
- The next morning, add rose oil and shake well to mix thoroughly.
- Pour it in a spritz bottle as use as a night toner.

Nothing better than ending the day with a splash of rose and jasmine before going to bed. You can use rose water to soak the jasmine and ditch the rose oil for the same results.

14. Face and Body Hair Removal

Although there's one DIY wax recipe in the Under-Three-Minutes Hacks section of this book, I felt like I should be spoiling my readers with choices. As you read more, you'll know what I'm talking about.

Lasers are expensive and waxing is painful, yet we have unwanted hair and we find a way to deal with it on special occasions. But guess what—there are ways to treat unwanted hair and reduce the growth over time.

I'm sure you can relate to those times when you do have the time but do not want to make a salon appointment. Many people hate human interaction so much that they'd rather contact an automated service or have Google clear their doubts as far as customer service is concerned. If you can relate to that statement, don't worry—you're not alone! I'm not too fond of too much interaction myself, but I do like troubleshooting my way out of things on my time and without breaking the bank. So here are a few DIY options for a girl's biggest struggle—hair removal.

a. Red Lentil *Ubtan* for Facial Hair

¼ cup milk
½ cup red lentil powder (*masoor* dal)
½ teaspoon wheat bran
1 teaspoon turmeric
1 teaspoon salt

- Add the red lentil powder, turmeric and salt to milk and mix thoroughly.
- In the direction of hair growth, apply the paste on your chin, side locks, upper lip and forehead with a spatula and let it dry. The thin layer will dry and look like wax.
- While you applied the paste in the direction of hair growth, while removing, make sure you roll out the pack *against* the hair growth direction.

This will not pull off your hair like wax does, but over time, applying this pack will slow down the growth and give you soft, radiant skin.

b. Hair-Removing Dough for Body Hair

½ cup milk
2 cups wholewheat flour
A few teaspoons almond oil
Use the flour and milk to make a dough.
Add almond oil and make a few mini-doughs out of it.

Use these mini doughs to roll over in the hairy portions of your arms, legs or even face to remove unwanted hair.

This hair-removing *ubtan* is great for infants just a few weeks old as well. Our ancestors have practised this for ages.

How toxic is a relationship where a person keeps apologizing after doing the same thing over and over again. Thinking you'll be the same as before and expecting you to withstand the whole thing.

Your skin feels the same way when you make it lack balance. You don't have to take away before you give it back. Don't dry it out completely before you pump the hydration back in. Don't deprive and then refill. Let your skin find solace in a routine that keeps it happy every minute, every second and not just pay attention to it only when it's crying out for help.

2

Eyes

I get it. You want to excel in your career, meet your soulmate and find the true happiness that you constantly look for. That requires you to answer a 12 a.m. mail from work, and a 2 a.m. text from your potential partner—which leads you to read between the lines for another couple of hours. What if I told you all this can happen organically without you losing your calm and being a night owl?

Get that #BeautySleep.

If you have to draw a pie chart of how long you need to do your make-up, I bet 95 per cent of the chart will be filled in the colour that represented your eyes, and it's mostly that winged eyeliner that people are still trying to master even when it's been a full decade of hard trying.

Poetry, love, quotes, stories and tutorials—why do eyes get more mentions than any other part of your body? From philosophy to practicality, eyes have special importance in every context. Soulful eyes, expressive eyes, sexy eyes, mysterious eyes . . . I don't think any other feature of your face can pull off as many adjectives as your eyes can. There's too much power in there, friends! Eyes even get to have more types of make-up techniques. Smokey eyes, gradient eyes, shimmery eyes, cat eye . . . you get the point!

So many styles and so much to master! There's a lot of suffering your eyes have to go through after all the chemical application, stress, polluted air and all the screen time, not to forget the lack of sleep. All that and we still don't thank our system enough to be so on point all the time.

And with concealers and other make-up products helping you conceal what our skin is trying to tell us, we've found comfort in living in denial. With this book, my goal is not only to help you fix skin issues holistically, but also make you listen to your body.

And when you're done taking notes and applying them to life, you'd embrace the minimal life where you are your best beautiful without concealers being involved.

From eyelashes to under eyes and more, having healthy, beautiful eyes can fully change the way you look.

Don't believe me? Try going to work without applying kohl and mascara. If you got a dime for each time someone asked you if you're sick, you'd be a millionaire by the end of the day.

Some may even call that make-up shaming, but the point is that it happens even when people mean well. But will that happen if you ditch your blush? Not much. Then what is it about the eyes that can transform your whole look?

You may enjoy saying that the bags under your eyes are Prada, and social media will make you think it's okay to be addicted to your phone, not have enough sleep, spend large chunks of time looking into your phone and do nothing about having panda eyes 'cause everyone else from our generation is having it . . .'

False! Your sight is an important sense that you should take full care of. Memes are mostly about being drunk, overweight, jobless and being a compulsive eater—none of which is healthy.

Every time I would get on a call with my mom to discuss my stress and skin concerns, she would immediately help me with some recipes that had simple ingredients . . . something every girl must have in her kitchen or garden. But one thing my mum (and your mum) would definitely not miss an opportunity to point out is the amount of time we spend in front of screens. TV, phone, office computer, laptop—when are we not sitting in front of a screen?

And it's not just the eyes. A research in *Zero Belly Diet*[1] even suggests that the more electronics we bring into the bedroom, the fatter we get! So, here it is . . . now we have every reason to listen to our moms.

---

[1] David Zinczenko, *Zero Belly Diet* (New York: Ballantine Books) 2014.

So divide your screen time evenly, have crazy beauty sleeps and power naps, and get the following DIY recipes in order to treat concerns and also relax your eyes.

DIY Almond Kohl

If you have a lady in the family who swears by home remedies, chances are that this has already been applied to your eyes as a kid. Our ancestors believed that kajal not only defines the eyes well, but applying it daily also shapes the eyes and makes them look bigger.

And since this recipe is made out of kitchen ingredients, it's hypoallergenic and safe to use for most people. If it's safe for a baby, it's safe for you . . . And why are we talking just safety? This kohl is far more efficient than all the 'natural' kohls out there.

4–5 almonds
2 forks
Fork stand
Brass plate (steel plate would also do)
A few drops of ghee

- Pierce the 2 almonds on 2 forks and hold them over the stove to burn them.
- Then make the forks with burning almonds stand tight on the stand. Almond burns easily as it has plenty of almond oil packed in it.

- Find two objects that can hold the brass plate right above the flames of those burning almonds so it's able to collect the black charcoal (produced out of the smoke of the burning almond) on the inside of the brass plate.
- Once the almonds are fully burnt, the inside of the plate will be all black when you lift it up. Careful! Don't lift if it seems too hot.
- Take a spoon and scrape the charcoal off the plate and put the powder in a steel bowl.
- Then add few drops of heated ghee on it and mix well.
- Your kohl is ready! You can use it as a regular kajal or an eyeliner. With the right kind of glitter layering this, eye pigments can also help you ace a smokey eye if need be!

1. Under-Eye Wrinkles

Lucky for us, we Indians face this problem quite late in the day as compared to people in the West or South. Our skin texture, on an average, is thicker, hence making it sag-proof to some extent till we're in our late thirties and early forties. After mid-twenties, when the production of collagen slows down in your body, ageing starts, even though it'll take some time to actually show.

But to delay that even more and fill your years with more youth, one can always be prepared with the right skincare regime.

Here are a few recipes to help you get rid of under-eye wrinkles:

a. Coffee Bean Powder + Extra Virgin Coconut Oil

2 teaspoons fine coffee bean powder
Few drops of extra virgin coconut oil

Love a cup of coffee to start the day? Save some to end the day too. Caffeine beats puffiness, and here's how you can use coffee to reduce under-eye bags.

- Mix 2 teaspoons fine coffee bean powder with few drops of extra virgin coconut oil to make an oily paste and apply under your eyes.
- After 15 minutes, separate the powder as it may feel coarse on the soft surface, and continue massaging the leftover oil till it's fully absorbed.
- You can rinse with a mild cleanser or go to sleep without washing (depends on what your skin is comfortable with).
- Practising this method twice a week can help you get rid of pigmentation, under-eye wrinkles and dry skin.

b. Fenugreek Leaves + Rosemary Oil

A handful of fenugreek leaves
Rosemary Oil

Fenugreek effectively reduces blemishes and fine lines on your face. These leaves, when mashed and mixed with an essential oil known for skin tightening—rosemary oil, make for a delicious-smelling under-eye pack.

- Keep it for 10–15 minutes and rinse to reduce blemishes and loose skin around your eyes.

c. Aloe Vera + Curd/Unflavoured Yogurt + Chamomile Tea Bags

Aloe vera
Curd/unflavoured yogurt
2 Chamomile tea bags

One of the reasons why people get under-eye bags is dryness. Aloe vera being rich in vitamins C, E and A (beta-carotene) is a great hydrant for the eyes, and the lactic acid in curd helps in skin lightening.

- Mix the aloe vera and curd and apply a light layer under your eyes.
- When your skin begins to absorb it, place freshly used chamomile tea bags (let them cool first) under the eyes.

When these ingredients are mixed and applied under the eyes, they not only help to get rid of puffiness, but also even your skin tone over time.

2. Dark Circles

There are so many causes for dark circles. Mostly stress and a poor sleep pattern lead to pigmentation in the skin. In the previous segment, I had given you some recipes that will soothe your eyes and help reduce under-eye circles. In this segment, I'll be focusing on the issue that most of us are trying to get rid of—dark circles.

Here are some easy recipes to take some load off you and help fix it.

a. Potato Juice + Mint Leaves

Potato juice has a natural bleaching agent that fights blemishes and discolouration; and mint has menthol, and is rich in vitamins A and C. Both of them combined make for an amazing combo of a pigmentation-fighting pack that you can apply on your eye area to lighten dark circles.

- Grate and extract the juice of half a potato.
- Crush some mint leaves and mix it with the potato juice.
- Apply under your eyes to treat pigmented skin around the eyes.

b. Cocoa + Avocado

Fat is good for restoring youth in your face. Avocado's fatty acids bring the good fat back to your face and under-eye area, if you have dark circles.

- Mix cocoa powder with warm water and set aside.
- Grind avocado slices to make a paste.
- Add 3 teaspoons of the cocoa water to the avocado paste and apply under your eyes to treat uneven skin and wrinkles. When you're in a hurry, applying a mashed avocado on your face is not bad.

c. Curd+ Cucumber Juice + Almond Oil

Curd evens the skin, and cucumber juice is soothing for the eyes. These two extracts when mixed with almond oil bring in the goodness of vitamins C, E and A and help combat panda eyes.

- Take half a teaspoon curd.
- Grate and extract the juice of half a cucumber and mix it with curd.
- Add a couple of drops of almond oil and mix it.
- Apply on the under-eye area to calm and relax the eyes and even the skin tone.

d. Buttermilk + Turmeric

We know raw milk helps discolouration, but buttermilk is even better to even your skin tone by fighting dark circles. And turmeric even acts as an under-eye concealer when mixed with buttermilk—but that's only for select skin tone groups. Do you know what's for all skin tone groups? This buttermilk and turmeric pack!

- Get 50 ml buttermilk and mix a pinch of turmeric with it.
- The pack would be thin as buttermilk is and needs to be applied like you'd apply any liquid solution and left on overnight.
- Try this 3–4 times a week to track the improvement.

3. Puffy Eyes

Puffed Eyes = Tired Eyes

Understandably, we have them as we are a generation of people who claim to be living a tired life.

Not to mention one of the sought-after rappers of our time even has 'Always Tired' tattooed below his eyes! Yes, I'm talking about Post Malone. It was so apt that another celeb (Rita Ora) won the 2018 Halloween, and the Internet, simply because she dressed up as him for Halloween, flaunting the same slogan under her eyes.[1]

#MidweekBlues, #Mondaze, #HumpDay, #Smonday . . . if you Google these hashtags, you'll know that these #s have something to do with the urge of getting close to the weekend and finding some time to do nothing at all and being proud of it. Our generation, which relates to coping with more exhaustion, stress, anxiety and competition than ever, has earned it.

---

[1] https://www.independent.co.uk/life-style/fashion/rita-ora-post-malone-halloween-costume-haunted-house-party-wembley-london-a8604161.html

Millennials in India are ranked as the 'most stressed in the world' by a survey conducted by Cigna TTK Health Insurance Company. Stats revealed that 95 per cent of Indian millennials between 18 and 34 years of age are stressed because of work, beating the global average, i.e. 86 per cent.[2]

Now that I've spilled the tea, here's how you can heal puffiness using tea bags.

Stuff that is cold causes the skin to shrink. That's how ice cubes are such an instant fix for open pores. Same is the case with cold tea bags. Caffeine beats puffiness and natural tannins in tea bags can make your life easier.

Change the fate of your used tea bag from living in a trash can to sitting on your eyes. For 15–20 minutes anyway.

When you take the tea bag out of the hot water cup, let it cool off for some minutes and then rest it on your eyes. You can also refrigerate them after steeping if you want to speed up the process. Here are the teas you can choose from:

a. Green Tea: Every kitchen has this. And if it's not helping you lose weight, get your money's worth by putting those bags into good use and redeeming the power of caffeine.

---

[2] https://economictimes.indiatimes.com/magazines/panache/ 95-millennials-stressed-in-india-work-is-the-main-trigger/ articleshow/65636099.cms

b. Black Tea: Black tea has more antioxidants than green tea, so don't limit your options when it comes to getting your dose of the same. Using black tea bags on your under eyes regulates blood flow and hence helps de-puff the eyes.

c. Chamomile Tea: It's the tea that calms you and helps you sleep. Its relaxing properties also make it a great option for treating red, tired eyes. In fact, it works out perfectly that you prepare a cup to sip before sleeping, and by the time you're done drinking it, the bag that has cooled off can be used to treat dark circles and puffiness.

4. Eyelashes

I'm the biggest mascara hoarder I know. Nothing finishes our eye make-up like a thick layer of mascara. You've probably read a quote for girls that said, 'I won't cry after you, my mascara is too expensive.' To which boys clap-backed and said, 'If your mascara is too expensive, it should've been waterproof!' *Boo, yeah*!

The point is, keeping your lashes healthy organically should be a major part of your beauty regime; layering it with mascara should *only* be the bonus.

Imagine being asked if you were wearing false lashes or clear mascara looking at you even when you're wearing none. I get that a lot, and it definitely feels amazing. It's surprising that almost every chapter in my book has everything to do with what my mom does, but when it comes to my long lashes, I think my brother and I take after our dad.

Some people have extremely long lashes even as toddlers—my Aussie niece Audrey being one case in point. It's unfair how some of us have to spend thousands getting lash extensions, while some didn't have to spend a dime. Lucky for us, holistic beauty has an answer to every problem and it's quite low-maintenance.

So, if you have fairly long lashes, this chapter is to help you on how to cleanse and maintain them, and if you're trying to grow them, here's how to do that as well!

Taking off mascara and false eyelashes before sleeping is crucial. Your lashes can be damaged if your face rubs on your pillow overnight. Make sure your eyes are devoid of any cosmetics before you sleep. Here are some oils and solutions you should apply to your lashes before you go to sleep to have long, voluminous lashes. The best way to apply these to your lashes is by a spare mascara wand . . . so make sure you start storing those. Mascara wands can be used for so many things—that's one thing you should never throw even when you toss the other half of it when the product is over. Wash and keep them to apply the following DIY lash serums and oils.

Make sure you apply a thin layer as you don't want a thick layer of anything on your eyes overnight.

i. Castor Oil + Vitamin E Oil

Consuming inexpensive Vitamin E capsules can treat a number of skin and hair problems. Applying the extracts of this capsule around your eyes (mixed with aloe vera gel or any cream that makes the extract less viscous) can help you treat dark circles and grow your lashes long and strong. In this case, it is better to mix Vitamin E capsule extract or oil with castor oil.

Castor oil itself is rich in Vitamin E and triglyceride—a variant of fatty acids that promote lash thickening, strengthening and lengthening.

ii. Olive Oil + Aloe Vera

What's better than one strong ingredient? Two strong ingredients that can hold hands to finish a job. These two ingredients are amazing even when applied separately. But combining the two makes it a sure-fire formula. Olive oil can help hair grow and so can aloe vera. Just pour a few drops on the bristles of the wand and rub it on a sliced open aloe leaf to mix the two. Apply on the lashes and sleep. This is something you can do 4–5 times or every day for best results.

iii. Green Tea + Coconut Milk

Same as above, they're okay to be used individually, but combining them is great for better results. Mascara wand or cotton earbuds, both can be used to apply a blend of these two to your eyes before sleeping. So the next time you sip green tea, save a few drops to mix with coconut milk to get those voluminous lashes in progress.

iv. Almond Oil + Argan Oil + Neem Oil

Pretty much most ingredients that are rich in Vitamin E and fatty acids can help you in this department. And there are no exceptions in this case. These three oils help hair growth, making it a great composition of a three-ingredient formula for longer eyelashes.

5. Eyebrow Serums

Wavy brow, feather brow, braided brow—the world has seen it all. Most of the bizarre beauty trends include brow play. The beauty industry is ready to show the weightage of having good brows. After thousands of brow pencils and pomades being launched every day, not to mention micro-needling treatments and brow waxing techniques, brows have become a big market now.

Sticking through thick and thin may have got a new meaning since brow transformations became all the rage. The way you do your brows can even influence what the shape of your face looks like. Not to mention how the Internet is full of sayings like, 'Don't let anyone with bad brows give you advice on life.'

In a day and age that gives so much weightage to brows and how the shape of it plays a role in giving a your face a lift, it's hardly original not to discuss the DIY recipes for lush brows naturally

a. Flax Seeds + Boiled Water + Sesame Seed Oil

Flax seeds have Vitamin E and so does sesame, with added B complex.

- Simmer half a cup flax seeds in boiling water till the flax seeds start dissolving and the water starts thickening.
- Keep stirring till the seeds become soft and the thick paste starts forming in the heating pan.
- Strain the paste and pour the solution in a bowl.
- When the solution cools off, you can add castor or Argan oil and apply the paste on your brows to help you grow defined, prominent brows overnight.

b. Fenugreek Seeds + Raw Milk

- Soak fenugreek seeds in water overnight and grind them the next morning.
- Mix raw milk to the paste and apply on your brows with a cotton earbud to up your brow game!

Now that we've got your eye routine in order, here are a few tips on how to see yourself:

- Don't let anyone influence the way you see yourself.
- Have a hard look at your day each night and be grateful for the little things and pretend the stressing stuff didn't happen.
- Stroke some eyeliner and tell the world you're up to win again, next morning.

3

Lips

You are a voice of reason. Lighting up a room with your wit and thoughts is just another day in your life. Every word out of your lips is savage. In the words of Elizabeth Taylor—'Pour yourself a drink, put on some lipstick, and pull yourself together.'

#YouGoGirl

Am I the only one who's sick of Kylie Jenner wannabes on social media? There are articles being written about how the Kardashians have impacted the beauty industry and influenced women to get more lip jobs and all. Writers are busy picturing and writing about how the perspective of beauty would change if the K-J *Clan* didn't exist.

In one of her interviews where Kylie admitted to getting lip injections, she said that she did it because she hated her natural lips and that no one wanted to kiss her. And now, she feels she doesn't need it any more.

Why? Because she thinks she could look beautiful without them. But unlike her, you don't have to wait for someone else to tell you whether you're kissable or not. In fact, your self-care and beauty routine doesn't have to be a slave to your dating life at all.

Injections are so out of context here, but I can't help but mention this one girl who went to get fillers and her case ended up going viral. And not for the right reasons. The fluid was accidentally injected into an artery and the result was scary . . .

I know you just Googled it!

The point is, if you ask ten people what they would like to change about their face, their answer would probably be nose or lips. But the world has seen enough surgery fails to fear it adequately.

Skin is in—so is authenticity, and realness.

I've seen vloggers rub wasabi on their lips to make them burn and swell to achieve a plumper look. And to be honest, over-drawn lips seemed such a sane idea compared to that. Nature has an answer to solve all your problems without harming or backfiring. So, read on to get all you lip fixes in this chapter.

1. Lip Scrubs

Pigmented, chapped and rough lips happen to all. Regular use of cosmetics, not wearing sunscreen on your lips and lack of exfoliation leads us to having these concerns.

Here are some DIY lip scrubs that will leave your lips looking pink, soft and supple. And leave an even canvas for your lip balm and lipstick to set on.

a. Lip Scrub + Moisturizer

1 teaspoon cream (*malai*)
A pinch of saffron (*kesar*)
A few rose petals (*desi gulab*)
¼ teaspoon white unbleached sugar

- Mix all ingredients together and rub gently on your lips for 5–7 minutes.
- After massaging, leave it on for another 10 minutes and wash.
- You can exclude the sugar and use the same recipe for a lip moisturizer.

b. Lip Tint-In-Moisturizer

A few drops of raw milk
A few drops of grated beetroot juice
A few drops of castor oil

In the chapter on eyes, I suggested you save your mascara wands to apply lash enhancing oils. In this chapter, I'm advising you to save your old lip gloss wands and clean them to apply these lip moisturizers.

Beetroot makes for an excellent natural lip and cheek tint. You can use it without adding anything else to add colour to your lips and go hours without having the burden of wearing chemicals on your lips. In fact, you can carry grated beetroot in your bag to extract juice and retouch your lips if you want to take a break from using lipsticks.

- Mix beetroot juice with raw milk and castor oil and apply to your lips using the gloss wand, any time of the day. This formula will nourish your lips, add colour to it and help depigment them.

c. Cocoa Lip Scrub

1 teaspoon raw milk
A pinch of coffee powder
A pinch of sugar

Coffee and sugar are natural exfoliators.

- Mix them with raw milk and scrub and shoo away chapped lips.
- Gently massage for 5 minutes and wash.
- Follow up with a lip balm.

d. Lip Depigmenting Mask

½ teaspoon water
1 pinch baking soda
A few drops of cucumber juice
A few drops of almond oil

- Baking soda has stain-removing and cleaning capabilities. Add it to water, along with cucumber juice and almond oil and wash it off after 3–4 minutes to reverse the effects of smoking and pollution showing on your lips.

2. DIY *Lip Balms*

The times we live in are awesome! We can customize and personalize anything we want. So it's high time we're applying the same to beauty. Following is a list of lip balm recipes you can make at home. I suggest, go mad over this and come up with plenty of options to use from every day.

a. Minted Rose Lip Balm

1 tablespoon beeswax
1 Vitamin E capsule
1 tablespoon cocoa butter
1 tablespoon rose oil
1 tablespoon peppermint oil

- Melt beeswax and let it cool a bit.
- Cut open the Vitamin E capsule and pour the extracts into the beeswax and throw the outer shell.
- Then add cocoa butter and let it cool down.
- Add rose oil and peppermint oil and mix everything well.
- Then pour the melted balm in a small pot container and freeze it to solidify it.

- Make sure the solution is a little warm when you freeze it, don't keep it super-hot though.

b. Lavender Lemongrass Lip Balm

1½ tablespoon beeswax
1 tablespoon coconut oil
1 tablespoon cocoa butter
1 tablespoon Vitamin E oil
1 tablespoon lemongrass oil
1 tablespoon lavender oil

- Melt the beeswax and add cocoa butter and coconut oil while it's still hot.
- Add Vitamin E, lavender and lemongrass oil and mix well.
- Pour it into the small container you wish to store the balm in.
- Freeze and solidify your lip balm.

Bonus: You can replace lemongrass and lavender with any two compatible essential oils of your choice to come up with your very own, special lip balm combo. A blend of 6 drops of essential oils per 30ml of carrier oil should be able to help you get most combinations correct.

c. Vanilla Coffee Lip Balm

1½ tablespoon beeswax
1 tablespoon coconut butter

2 tablespoons coffee-infused oil
1 teaspoon vanilla extract

- Melt beeswax and add coconut butter, coffee-infused oil and vanilla extract.
- Pour it in a box and freeze to solidify.

Now that you have fantastic looking lips, let's discuss your power of speech. The words that come out of your mouth, need to compete with the outer beauty:

- Us millennials may have more sarcastic comebacks but we're also the wise ones. When you're a true voice of reason, at home, workplace, and beyond, you're wise! When you're not around, let people miss THAT side of you. You'll know how much more you'll feel wanted by others!

4

Neck

Hold your head high. Get your girls to do the same. Being the girl that you are isn't easy. Fighting the fights you fight isn't either. Show them the gracefully unapologetic lady you've become. #ChinUpPrincess or the crown slips!

I've read articles on beauty and watched videos in my free time all my life, but never do people ever talk about taking care of your neck that often.

Of the many signs that'll give away your age no matter how you're defying it otherwise is your hands and neck . . . if one's that creepy to notice it, that is. The lines on your neck start thickening with age.

The neck is quite ignored till the time we pull out our favourite swimsuit, halter neck blouse or backless dress. Only then do we care about blending foundation, highlighting or even moisturizing that area.

This just hit you, didn't it?

Don't worry—it's not too late for anything. The only common problem this area deals with is fine lines and wrinkles. And here's how you save the base of your face.

1. Potato Juice + Lemon Juice + Rose Water

¼ cup Potato juice
2 tablespoons lemon juice
Rose water

Potato juice reduces fine lines and evens skin tone. Lemon juice has plenty of Vitamin C. Rose water refreshes your skin by balancing its pH levels.

- Mix fresh potato juice with 2 tablespoons of lemon juice and rose water. Apply to neck for about 30 minutes before jumping in the shower.
- Wash off, or you can even bathe after applying this.

The best way to use these neck masks is to apply them before you go to take a bath.

2. Cabbage Juice + Honey + Ylang Ylang Oil

½ cup cabbage juice
1 tablespoon honey
A dash of ylang ylang oil

Cabbage has skin-tightening capabilities, ylang ylang oil boosts skin proteins and promotes cell renewal, and honey smoothens the skin.

- Extract ½ cup worth of cabbage juice.
- Add a tablespoon of honey and a splash of ylang ylang oil.
- Mix well and apply this liquid paste on your neck area and rinse when it dries.
- Repeat twice or thrice a week.

3. Egg White + Turmeric + Orange Juice

1 egg white
1 teaspoon orange juice
¼ teaspoon turmeric powder

Neck wrinkles are not much different from face wrinkles. One can use egg whites for the neck the same way it is used for facial wrinkles and fine lines.

- Crack an egg and separate the egg white from the yolk.
- Add 1 teaspoon orange juice and ¼th teaspoon turmeric and mix well.
- Apply a layer of this on your neck in upward motion and rinse when it dries.
- Use twice or thrice a week.

4. Chickpea Flour + Curd + Rosehip Oil

2 tablespoons of chickpea flour
1½ tablespoons of curd
5–6 drops of rosehip oil

Rosehip oil helps reduce fine lines and scars. Curd fights discolouration and chickpea flour tightens the skin.

- Mix 2 tablespoons of chickpea flour and add it with 1½ tablespoons of curd and mix well.
- Add 5–6 drops of rosehip oil and apply the paste to your neck and let it dry.
- Rinse and moisturize.

5. Yogurt + Black Seed Oil + Olive Oil

1 teaspoon black seed oil
1 teaspoon olive oil
¼ cup yogurt

The lactic acid in yogurt helps even skin tone and tighten skin. Olive oil helps reduce the appearance of fine lines. Black seed oil, also known as black cumin seed oil, repairs free radicals that cause the skin to age and develop wrinkles.

- Add 1 teaspoon black seed oil and 1 teaspoon olive oil to ¼ cup of yogurt.

- Apply to your neck and rinse with water, when it's mostly absorbed.
- Repeat twice or thrice a week.

You can also use avocado oil or extract if you can't get black seed oil.

Feel free to add tomato juice to all ingredients in the list to de-tan skin around your neck.

You've found new ways to hold your head high over a fab neck, but here's how your state of mind will be:

- When integrity is non-negotiable for you, you'll bypass every problem with grace.
- When you declare that your self-esteem is your biggest priority, you'll have it your way and be respected for it.
- Sure, you may have to allow people to get used to your ways, but when you get a hang of it, it'll be your high and nothing average will either interest or impress you.

5

Hair

Wind in your hair, fire in your soul. Can they ever handle the #GoodHairDay you? You slay at a work meeting, rock a first date, get what you want while having a good hair day. You're nicer when you like your hair, aren't you?

Frankly, I think the power of good hair is *still* underrated even when phrases such as 'good hair days' and 'bad hair days' are a part of daily conversations. How you're going to wear your hair is planned in advance for every important occasion. From shampooed hair to third-day (greasy hair) styles, all of us give a fair amount of thought to how we do our hair while planning a look.

From feather hair and big hair from the '50s to slick back ponytails of 2019, playing with volume and texture has proven how the volume and density of hair can change the game. The viral beauty videos feature all those over-the-top unattainable hair art, leaving us, from time to time, thirsty to simply achieve just regular luscious hair, if nothing crazy.

Honestly, we deserve a support group for handling all the tantrums of our hair. We get it set in a certain way, right when it's time to step out and meet people, but more importantly, when finally taking pictures, it looks like something else. The curls open while the night is still young, and the straightened hair becomes frizzy before your shift got over . . . like we didn't have enough things to control already.

With lack of time and motivation, some of us give up and go to work without spending too much time on how we wear our hair and then end up posting an Insta story saying stuff like, 'Bad hair don't care'—which we clearly lie about . . . it's impossible not to care. Or at least it is for someone's who's reading this book right now.

But, denial ain't good for you, girl, when looking the best and feeling the best has been the motto all along.

When the mane is the main concern, it's best to be prepared for all challenges. So, be it pollution, heat or cold, this chapter will not only focus on the basic concerns of haircare, but also throw light on a haircare regime that you should be adopting quite early on to have a strong hair game for as long as you can.

1. Hair Growth Boosting Water

This may just be one of the easiest techniques in the book, but it's super rare and surprising.

This two-ingredient hair growth water acts as a miracle solution for your hair growth plans.

Water + Dodders (*Amar Bel*)

Dodders is a parasitic plant that is a member of the 'Morning Glory' family and belongs to the Cuscuta group. It forms anchoring roots to grow in a rapid phenomenon until it reaches a host plant. Blooming between April and July, it is in this plant's nature to grow and spread. In the concept of Ayurveda, this plant has proven to multiply the generation of follicles to prevent hair fall.

- Cut and dip a few hundred grams of this plant in hot water for 20 minutes and let it cool off. Then sieve the plant out of the water and keep aside.
- After your regular shampoo and conditioning rinse, go with the last and final rinsing with this water.
- Repeat thrice a week for your hair to grow faster than ever.

2. *Scalp Buildup Exfoliating Scrub*

1½ tablespoon brown sugar
½ tablespoon avocado oil
½ tablespoon coconut oil
A few drops of lemon juice (½ lemon)

Scalp buildup is a common hair concern. Just like your lips and face need exfoliation to breathe and make your make-up last longer, your scalp also needs scrubbing and exfoliation to feel fresh and keep excess oil at bay. This nourishing scrub will help you achieve exactly that.

If your scalp is too dry or too oily, this may help bring just the right amount of oil balance to make your life easy.

- Mix all ingredients in a bowl and apply to dry hair.
- Scrub your scalp thoroughly but gently, and leave it on for 20–30 minutes.
- Rinse with a shampoo, followed by your favourite conditioner.
- Repeat twice or thrice a week to reduce scalp buildup and dullness over time.

3. Hair Masks

Dandruff, flakiness, scalp acne, dryness, hair growth, premature greying—here's a mask for every concern.

Greasy scalp leads to loss of volume. I have been there where your scalp feels oily just a day after you shampooed—twice. And that has led me to believe that shampooing your scalp twice or thrice at once will not cut it.

Walking away from shampoos that have sulphate and masking your scalp to fulfil its needs is the way to go. Oily scalp behaves the way it does not because it has too much oil, but because it's too dry and craving some hydration—the way it is with your skin.

I've got hair mask recipes for those who are facing the exact opposite of this situation and more. Try to mask your hair once or twice a week for best results.

a. To Treat Oily Roots/Flaky Scalp

MASK 1

People who have oily roots often complain about having a flaky scalp that makes all the freshness go away the very next day after the head wash. If your scalp produces excess sebum, you know what I'm talking about. Here's how you can address that problem and control it with some very easily available ingredients:

2 teaspoons *ritha* powder
2 teaspoons *amla* powder
2 teaspoons *shikakai* powder
2 teaspoons multani mitti powder
10 drops lemon juice (always skip this ingredient if you have coloured hair)
1 cup aloe vera
2 tablespoons tea leaves simmered in water

Amla is a natural anti-oxidizing agent that gives your scalp stem cell therapy—a process that helps generate new hair and prevents hair from greying. Ritha, also a rich source of more antioxidants, happens to be packed with iron. All these mixed with shikakai and lemon juice (both bringing loads of Vitamin C to the table) make for a perfect paste for the ultimate weekly scalp cleanse.

- Mix all ingredients together to create a paste.
- And while preparing the paste, simmer 2 tablespoons of tea leaves in water for 15 minutes and keep it aside to cool off. You'll need the tea solution after you're done applying the paste to your hair.
- Apply the paste on your scalp and wait for 25–30 minutes. This paste will not lather like your regular shampoo, but will totally clean your scalp leaving it fresher for longer.
- If your scalp is super, super oily, you can use a mild shampoo to rinse off this mask.
- After you're done rinsing, use the tea leaf water as your hair conditioner. Unlike the regular conditioner you can work your way up to the scalp with this, as tea leaves won't make your scalp oily. In fact, it'll actually help reduce dandruff and make your hair more smooth and manageable.

For normal scalp, the same ingredients need to be used with a further addition of hibiscus leaves, curry leaves, henna leaves and ber *leaves (Indian jujube/zizyphus mauritiana) to make your hair more luscious than ever.*

MASK 2

4 cloves of garlic
A few drops of eucalyptus oil
10-12 mint leaves
8-10 drops of lemon juice
1 cup curd

Garlic works as a natural antifungal agent, even for acne. It'll refresh your scalp along with the mint, lemon and curd that'll make for a complete formula for scalp cleaning. To keep excess oil at bay, eucalyptus oil comes in to control your scalp sebum. And to fully condition your scalp in a way that's best for it, curd takes up the job.

- Crush the garlic cloves and grind the mint leaves.
- Add some curd, extract of 2 lemons and top the paste with a few drops of eucalyptus oil.
- Apply the mask to your scalp 20 minutes before cleansing with a mild shampoo.

MASK 3

Apple cider vinegar
½ teaspoon baking soda
Few drops of tea tree oil
Handful of rosemary leaves
Handful of mulberry leaves (*shehtoot*)

All these ingredients have a way of banishing scalp greasiness and oil.

- Crush a handful of mulberry and rosemary leaves.
- Add apple cider vinegar just enough to not make the paste too watery.
- Add ½ teaspoon baking soda and a few drops of tea tree oil.

- Apply the paste to your scalp for 20 minutes before you rinse with a gentle cleanser.

b. For a Dry Scalp

People with oily scalp wish to have a dry scalp sometimes. That is because their shampoo session means nothing by the end of day when all the oil makes a comeback. The grass on the other side always seems greener. But if you ask people with dry scalp, it isn't pretty for them either. Dandruff always sitting on your shoulder and combs that feel like they're painfully scratching your head? Dry scalp has its own share of challenges that can be fixed with these easily available hair mask recipes. These recipes are also effective in managing dandruff, although there's a separate chapter for it ahead. So, mask away your dry scalps with these nourishing ingredients!

MASK 1

2 bananas
2 tablespoons of honey
¼ cup cucumber juice

Banana and honey can condition your scalp without making it oily, and cucumber can add freshness to it.

- Slice up and mash 2 bananas well and mix 2 tablespoons of honey and cucumber juice just enough to make it a semi-solid paste.

- Apply the mask and let it sit for 20–30 minutes before you wash it with a gentle shampoo followed by your conditioner.

MASK 2

4 slices of pineapple
4 drops lavender oil
½ sliced avocado

Pineapple has anti-inflammatory properties that are capable of soothing a dry scalp and avocado, with its fatty amino acids and antioxidant vitamins acts as a natural moisturizer for your scalp.

- Put 4–5 slices of pineapples and avocados in a grinder and grind it for just a few seconds. Make sure the paste doesn't look like a juice but a paste.
- Add lavender oil and apply the paste to your scalp to keep frizz and scalp dryness at bay.
- Keep this mask on for 30 minutes before rinsing with a shampoo.

MASK 3

2 tablespoons of mayonnaise
1 egg
A few drops of olive oil

Mayonnaise fights dryness and frizziness and egg brings protein and lustre to your hair. The olive oil is to retain moisture.

- Crack an egg and pour the yolk and white in a bowl.
- Add the 2 tablespoons of mayonnaise and a few drops of olive oil.
- Mix these ingredients well and apply on your scalp.
- Keep it on for 30 minutes before washing with a shampoo.

Now, the smell of eggs could be an issue and it's not something you can get rid of easily. But things we do for good hair, right? Don't worry I'm not asking you to live with it. For you already have the will, let me show you the way(s). Apply one of these ingredients to your scalp and hair to help manage the smell: fresh lemon juice, fresh orange juice, Vinegar (mix 2 teaspoons with 1 cup of water)

MASK 4

1 cup buttermilk
½ cup black soil (*kaali mitti*)

- Soak black soil in buttermilk overnight and wash your hair with the buttermilk-soaked black soil for a nurturing cleanse and conditioning.

- Leave it on for half an hour and wash normally.
- You may not need to follow up with a shampoo or conditioner after this—the mask is that efficient.

This two-ingredient recipe can eliminate oil, impurities and bring lustre back to your hair.

> *The ghee made out of cow milk is also the greatest frizz-managing, detangling agent for your hair. Just applying that to your hair will help you feed your scalp, tame unruly hair and beat dullness.*

4. Dandruff

Dandruff is a casual term, but will you be more scared of it if I tell you that it's caused by a fungus? Because it is! *Malassezia*, a type of fungus that thrives on and consumes the natural oils (sebum) that your scalp produces is the reason behind dandruff. That means oiling your hair with any random oil could be a wrong decision, unless the ingredients have dandruff-banishing properties.

Apart from smaller concerns of it falling on your shoulders and ruining your looks, there are more serious concerns to having dandruff. The worst part is that it gets worse around that time of the year when it's difficult to take a head wash every day—winters!

But if you prep yourself through the year to fight these concerns, the problem can be managed by using the following DIY hair masks.

MASK 1

½ cup *ber* powder (Indian jujube)
Aloe vera
A few drops of glycerine

I just Googled 'ber' to find all its other names only to find that this super fruit is quite a diva![1]

It is also known as: Chinese Apple, Jujube, Indian Plum, Masau, Korean Dates, Chinese Dates, Red Dates and Indian Dates. But, don't let that confuse you! Ber is a humble fruit that has antioxidants, Vitamin C, phytonutrients and flavonoids that are great for your skin and hair. Eating it or applying it, both can do wonders for your skin and scalp.

Adding to that is another itchiness and flakiness fighting component—aloe vera—that helps reduce sebum, further making your fight against dandruff more effective.

- Slice up an aloe stem and extract the pulp and mash it.
- Add ber powder and mix well.
- Add 10 drops of glycerine—that'll help your scalp ease up on the irritation and flakiness.
- Repeat 2–3 times a week, or before every head wash.

---

[1] https://hort.purdue.edu/newcrop/morton/indian_jujube.html

MASK 2

1 cup green tea leaves or green tea
3 teaspoons white vinegar
½ teaspoon coconut oil

Coconut oil hydrates the scalp; white vinegar helps balance your scalp's pH levels; and like *ber*, green tea also has antioxidants. So, whether you crush the used green tea leaves or use actual liquid green tea, both can help you banish dandruff and frizz in this case.

- Mix green tea, coconut oil and white vinegar to create a pre-shampoo hair mask-in-oil and then shampoo 30 minutes after application.
- Repeat before whenever you plan a head bath.

MASK 3

½ cup bentonite clay
2 teaspoons wheat germ oil
1 melted camphor
¼ cup cucumber juice

A great summer hair mask, as bentonite clay, cucumber juice and camphor are cooling agents to your scalp. Just like coconut oil, wheat germ oil will also condition your hair to make it less flaky.

- Mix bentonite clay, wheat germ oil, melted camphor and cucumber juice in a bowl to make a paste and apply to your scalp.
- Rinse after 15–20 minutes, followed by a mild shampoo.
- Repeat once a week.

5. Hair Conditioning and Polishing

Protecting your hair from sun damage and sleeping on silk pillowcases are not the only easy fixes you can do to get shiny hair. Your hair that's deprived of lustre is craving oil, nourishment and moisturization. As busy as our schedules may be, listening to our grandma/mama and oiling our hair before shampooing will always be the hero of all haircare advice. It's an oldie but a goldie. Speaking of which, here's how to help you get your hair to shine like gold:

15 hibiscus flowers
15 hibiscus leaves
15 neem leaves
15 curry leaves
15 henna leaves
5 amlas
A jar of coconut oil

- Collect all the ingredients listed above. Chop (or grate) the amlas and mix all the ingredients in a jar filled with coconut oil.

- Place the jar at a corner or near a window that gets decent sunlight. Don't expose it to direct sunlight.
- Close the lid of the jar and leave it for 1–2 months.

Yes, you read that correctly. It's important that we extract the maximum goodness out of all the ingredients and the results will be worth it. And considering it'll be a big jar (probably 2–3 litres) that can accommodate 15 leaves of each of the ingredients, you know it'll have enough oil to have your haircare fix in place for another year, so a couple of months to wait for the oil preparation doesn't sound like a bummer any more, does it?

- Once your hair oil is ready, pour it into a lined fabric set on top of a large bowl to use as strainer.

When you're done separating oil from other ingredients, you'll unlock your way to having a good hair year rather than settling for just good hair days.

This oil has to be heated and massaged into your roots and ends. Doing so will help fix dullness, and bring shine back to your hair that pollution and stress has deprived it of.

6. Hair Growth/Thickening, Root Strengthening, Preventing Premature Balding

I was quite the Rapunzel myself a year ago. I may have shoulder-length hair now, when I'm writing this book, but until last year I had knee-length hair . . . and funny but true, that may be more than half my height. So far, I've never faced troubles growing my hair, but then, I may consciously don't know so, but the reason behind it could be all those years of oiling my mother had done to my hair when I was younger. Every window in the house that has sun exposure had a huge glass container filled with some kind of oil in my house. I think it's safe to say that my mom is mad about oils. And for every hair concern, she has a recipe. Long or short, I've changed hairstyles all my life and what I get a lot is how I'm able to change it so quickly.

Most girls in my squad, family and office at some point, have joked about losing the craze of having long hair till the time they're actually able to grow it. It's true that you can't have the longest hair by the end of the week if you want, but these recipes may just help you grow your desired length while you're still in that phase.

So, here it goes!

a. Oil-in-Mask 1

3 tablespoons sunflower seeds
3 tablespoons flax seeds
2 tablespoons pumpkin seeds
Half a bunch of coriander leaves
Few drops of olive oil

- Mix the coriander leaves, sunflower seeds, flax seeds and pumpkin seeds in a grinder and grind till it forms a thick paste.

- Then add a couple of drops of olive oil and mix well.
- Use this before a mild hair cleanse each time.

This particular mask is packed with hair growth-boosting ingredients. If you're serious about growing your hair fast, this should be your ultimate go-to.

b. Oil 1

4 onions
6 teaspoons neem oil/ghee
3 slices of aloe vera

Onion juice is best for those suffering with premature balding as it promotes new hair growth.

- Grind 4 onions in a grinder and extract the juice out in a bowl.
- Add neem oil, melted camphor and mashed aloe vera extract to the onion juice.
- Apply this oil-in-mask to your roots and leave it on for 45 minutes before you rinse it.

c. Oil 2

3 ridge gourds (*Turai*: *Luffa acutangula*)
2 litre coconut oil/sesame oil

- Peel and slice the 3 ridge gourds into small bits and let them dry for a day or two.

- When the vegetable has fully dried, simmer it in coconut or sesame oil.
- Leave the sliced vegetable in the oil for 60 minutes after you're done heating, then pour through a lined fabric or an oil strainer placed over a jar you plan on storing the oil in.
- And your oil is ready!

Applying this oil twice a week not only helps your hair grow faster, but also makes it denser. This oil is also capable of keeping your hair from greying in the long run, when used regularly. And since we've used litres of oil to make this, this much oil should get you through months easily.

d. Oil 3

6–7 banyan roots
2 cups of mustard oil (as required)
3 teaspoons sesame seeds

Banyan roots are an ancient remedy for hair loss and are easily available in the market, so it's a relief that you don't have to pull some out from the branches, but you could. If you do end up pulling one out, make sure to wash it off thoroughly and clean the dirt off it.

- Put the roots in a grinder and grind it for 7–8 seconds—just enough to not totally crush it.
- Simmer the mustard oil and add the roots and sesame seeds to it.

- When the roots look like they're drained, turn off the heat.
- Filter the mixture through a sieve and pour it into a jar.

This can be stored for a couple of uses before you make it again. Repeating this twice or thrice a week can help you grow longer hair in a short span.

7. *Premature Greying Treatment Oil*

1½ cups sesame oil
15 false daisies (*bhringraj*)
15 water hyssop (*brahmi*)
4 sliced Indian gooseberries (*amla*)

- Simmer the ingredients for half an hour in sesame oil without burning the ingredients.
- Strain and filter the ingredients out of the oil and keep it aside. And your oil is ready.

This oil strengthens roots and help treat premature greying.

8. *Hair Thickening and Conditioning Oil*

2 ½ cups almond oil
2½ cups coconut oil
2½ cups sesame oil
4 hibiscus flowers
15–20 hibiscus leaves

15 curry leaves
15 rose petals (*desi gulab*)
15 Indian jujube leaves (*ber patti*)
1 lemon
5 bags of green tea/½ cup green tea leaves

- Mix and heat all the oils (sesame, almond, coconut) and store them in a glass jar.
- Crush all the other ingredients (hibiscus, hibiscus leaves, curry leaves, rose petals, lemon and green tea leaves) thoroughly and dip in the jar full of mixed oils and shut the lid.
- Place the jar near a window that gets decent sun exposure and leave it for a week.
- Then filter the ingredients out of the oil after a week and start using the oil. This jar of oil will last for months.

This oil will thicken your hair and condition it. The remains of the filtered oil can be ground in a blender and used as a hair mask too!

9. Split Ends/Breakage

Splits are the worst. Whether it's your relationship or your hair, both need constant care to stand the test of time. Breakage and split ends can happen because of various reasons.

Using too many chemicals, or heat-based styling, not using enough oils or conditioners, or general carelessness—split ends and breakage are obvious signs of your hair being weak. Sometimes, not trimming your hair can also make the tips of your hair split, causing them to break.

Here's how you can avoid that situation by using these DIY oils:

a. Oil 1

1 cup mustard oil
15 neem leaves
30 henna leaves
30 holy basil (*tulsi*) leaves
1 10-cm aloe vera stem

- Mix neem, henna and basil leaves and the aloe vera stem in a grinder and grind it to make a paste.
- Simmer 1 cup mustard oil and add the paste and let it heat for 15 minutes.
- Let it cool and apply it to your hair to boost your hair strength and shine.
- Apply it twice or thrice a week overnight or hours before shampooing.

b. Oil 2

1 cup sesame oil (for rough hair) or coconut oil (for normal hair)
3 teaspoons castor oil

1 Vitamin E capsule
3 gooseberries, sliced and grated

- Simmer the sesame/coconut oil and add the grated gooseberries and castor oil to it.
- Filter and pour it in a bowl and break open a Vitamin E capsule and extract its contents into the bowl.
- Mix well and apply this oil to your hair to bond it and prevent it from splitting.
- Apply it twice or thrice a week overnight or hours before shampooing—whatever's suitable for your hair type.

10. Hair Straightening

Too many of us go for chemically straightened hair that only shows its true results once it starts wearing off. Suddenly your hair is wavy and curly from the roots and straighter from the tips and you have no idea which shampoo to use because every strand of your hair looks like it's from two different zip codes. We often redo the treatments, which further causes hair to start thinning over time, among other consequences.

Although there's no way to make hair poker straight, without using chemicals there's a better way to make your hair smoother and manageable. Fake a straighter texture by using these oils.

a. Oil 1

1 cup ghee/neem oil
15 ber leaves
15 hibiscus leaves
4–5 sliced aloe vera extracts

- Mix the ber, hibiscus and 2–3 aloe vera pieces and grind them to make a paste and keep aside.
- Simmer the ghee/neem oil for 10 mins and add the paste and apply it to your scalp.
- Comb your hair while it's oiled.
- Use the remaining sliced aloe vera extract to mix in your shampoo.
- When you're done shampooing and conditioning the hair, comb it when it's slightly wet till it's dry. This will make your hair look straighter and super manageable.

b. Mask 1

¾ cup olive oil
1 avocado

- Apply a thin layer of olive oil on your scalp.
- Slice and grind one avocado to make a paste and apply it over that thin layer of olive oil directly.
- Comb your hair and leave it for 20–30 minutes before washing it with a mild shampoo and conditioning it.

- You can detangle and comb your hair away from the roots while the conditioner is still on, pour water on it to cleanse it without tangling it with your hands.
- Once your hair is fully rinsed, dry it with a towel and them comb your damp hair with a wide-toothed comb.
- Apply serum only on the tips to have straighter, manageable hair all day.

11. Hair Serums

There's a serum for everything—body, hair, eye, face and even hands. But if you ask your mother if she needed a hair serum when she was 16, the answer would probably be no. Those days, even the first-generation shampoos were efficient enough to do the job of a conditioner and serums and everything beyond. But there's something about present times—our body suddenly develops the need for new products available in the market. And what's intriguing? Our body has a way of telling us how our routine is incomplete without those products. Hair serum is one of those products that are suddenly needed by everyone, especially for their hair. And how can you ever say no to something that makes your hair manageable and makes it smell delicious!

From banishing frizz to detangling and helping style your hair, these DIY serums will help give the perfect post-shampoo care your hair needs, and with these delicious smelling ingredients, you can use them as hair mists as well. As scalp can hold a fragrance for longer than other parts of the skin, use these moderately on the tips of damp hair as a serum, and spray it 15 cm away from a damp scalp to use them as hair mists.

a. Serum/Mist 1

1 cup distilled water
¾ cup aloe vera gel
A few drops of castor oil
A few drops of lavender oil
A few drops of peppermint oil

Castor oil helps grow your hair longer. Best for calming your senses, lavender oil will leave your hair smelling amazing too. And with all the freshness of peppermint, this overall makes for a great post shampoo serum for your hydration needs.

- Grind the aloe vera paste in grinder to make it finer.
- Add that aloe paste to distilled water along with a few drops of lavender, peppermint and castor oil.
- Pack this in a spray or a pump bottle and shake well before using.
- Spray a moderate quantity on your palm and apply evenly to your hair after shampooing.

b. Serum/Mist 2

1 cup rose water

A few drops of rosemary oil
A few drops of Vitamin E oil
A few drops of cedar wood oil

Rosemary and Vitamin E oil boost shine and hair growth. When mixed with rose water, it makes for a good recipe to feed your hair with the care it needs after a shampoo sesh. Cedar wood oil, apart from smelling amazing, is also capable of boosting hair quality.

- Fill the spray or pump bottle with rose water and add the oils.
- Apply to wet hair to detangle and smoothen your hair texture.

c. Serum/Mist 3

½ cup glycerine
A few drops of jasmine oil
A few drops of neroli oil
A few drops of grapeseed oil

Apart from smelling incredible, jasmine and neroli fight dull hair. Glycerine and grapeseed fight frizziness without making your hair greasy.

- Mix these ingredients in a spray bottle and apply in moderation to damp hair and brush it to get a manageable, delicious, luscious mane.

d. Serum/Mist 4

½ cup rose water
½ cup distilled water
A few drops of sandalwood oil
A few drops of patchouli oil

Sandalwood and patchouli oils make a great pair and, due to their strong smell, will probably last longer when sprayed to your scalp as a mist or to your tips as a serum.

- Mix rose water with distilled water and all the oils in a spritz bottle to make this amazing serum.

12. DIY Hair Colour Spray

Okay this is not your regular hair colour that bleaches the hair and leaves it dry, in splits. Dry and damaged hair is a pain I'd put no one through. These are healthy hair pigments that'll add a great hue of brunette and red to your natural colour because I wouldn't recommend any other colour for Indian skin. Brunette and mild reds match us the best. Although this will require some days and regular spray application to show results, the upside is that these are all ingredients that'll benefit the quality of your hair.

a. Hint of Red Spray Colour 1

1½ cups water
5 hibiscus flowers

5 calendula flowers
5 tablespoons beetroot juice

- Boil the water and steep the flowers in it for half an hour.
- Then extract the flowers completely from the water and put them away.
- Add beetroot juice to the water and store in a spray bottle and apply to your hair regularly.

b. Hint of Brunette Spray Colour 2

1½ cups water
5 rosemary leaves
1 tablespoon saffron
20 nettle leaves
20 sage leaves

- Boil the water and steep the saffron and nettle leaves in it for half an hour.
- Then strain all ingredients and put them away.
- Let the water cool down and pour it in a spray bottle.
- Spray regularly for weeks to see your hair change colour.

c. Highlight Renewing Spray 3

½ cup water
4 chamomile tea bags
A few drops of lemon juice

If you already have highlighted hair and are too lazy to go for a touch-up to make it seem new again, don't worry, there's a calming ingredient that'll fix this for you. Chamomile can turn a bad day around when you drink it before sleeping, but what it can also do is boost the colour of your highlights. Here's how:

- Boil the water and add chamomile tea bags to it and let it simmer for 30 minutes.
- Squeeze out the tea from the tea bags and put them away.
- Add a few drops of lemon to add freshness and store in a spray bottle.
- Spray to your hair regularly to keep your highlights look like you've just stepped out of a salon.

13. Herbal Shampoos

While I'm at suggesting tips to combat every hair problem, it's impossible to leave the most mandatory product out of the list. It's probably the one item you may have done a lot of experimentations with too. I know some people who rinse their hair combining two different shampoos, just to avail the goodness of both because the brand didn't make one that has both ingredients in the same bottle. It is that kind of situation where you end up buying two pairs of blush palettes just because the ones you liked are paired with different colours. Well, make no mistake, it's all smart strategy. How else can they bill you for two products when you needed one, otherwise?

But I'm one of those people who think it's high time we have our cake and eat it too.

And all our haircare needs should find a way to fit inside one bottle, because God knows we already have enough things to take care of.

I've seen my mom and aunt make their own shampoos since I was 10 or so. This segment will include hair ingredients for different scalp and hair types where one easily available ingredient—castile soap—is the constant ingredient that will help generate lather and clean your scalp. So, are we ready to put some good thoughts on our head?

a. Shampoo 1

½ cup chamomile tea leaves or 6–7 chamomile tea bags
½ cup castile soap
½ tablespoon glycerine
A lemon
1 cup distilled water

People dealing with anxiety and stress are advised to drink this tea before bed as it calms the brain. Its calming properties remain intact even when applying it to your scalp. If you have coloured hair or highlights, this relaxing shampoo can help boost that too.

Boil distilled water on high temperature and add chamomile tea bags/leaves in it. Filter and pour the tea in a bowl and discard the leaves/used tea bags. Then add lemon, glycerine and castile soap to the tea and store in a bottle once it cools off. Apply and use as any regular shampoo.

b. Shampoo 2

½ cup distilled water
½ teaspoon virgin coconut oil
½ cup coconut milk
1 teaspoon castor oil
A few drop of sandalwood oil
¼ cup castile soap

- Boil the distilled water and put it aside to cool off.
- Boil the coconut oil and add coconut milk, castor oil, sandalwood oil, castile soap and distilled water to it.
- Store it in a bottle after cooling and use it as a regular shampoo.

This scalp-cooling shampoo will help your hair grow faster while really nourishing it because of the presence of castor and sandalwood oils paired with coconut milk.

c. Shampoo 3

½ cup green/black tea leaves *or* 6–7 green/black tea bags
½ cup castile soap

½ tablespoon glycerine
1 cup distilled water
A few drops of cedar wood oil

Green and black tea, both are high on antioxidants. Black tea helps make your hair denser and green tea helps reduce hair loss. It's up to you which tea to choose.

- Dip the tea bags or leaves in hot water for half an hour and keep it aside till it cools off.
- Remove the tea bags or tea leaves and add castile soap, glycerine, few drops of cedar wood oil.
- Store the mixture in a bottle.

Cedar wood stimulates the scalp and smells incredible. Leaving this shampoo on for a few minutes before rinsing will improve scalp condition and make your hair smell amazing.

Natural Conditioner

This is a one-ingredient recipe! After shampooing, apply non-synthetic vinegar to your hair and leave it for 5 minutes and rinse. This process will give you the silkiest hair without any drama!

You have gorgeous hair, it's safe to say you have all the powers in the world to get you closer to your goals. Keeping your head and scalp fresh add super-powers to your day.

So no matter how lazy your are, get that scalp cleanse out of the way and your difficulties will clear your way organically. You have now found a way to unleash your inner Supergirl everyday. You're welcome!

6

Body

As they rightly say, 'In a society that profits from your self-doubt, loving yourself is a rebellious act.' Be that rebel and turn it all around. Make sure you love you and everything about you. Be #HeadOverHeels about yourself.

None of the ancient practices in Indian context exist without a reason. In ancient times, scholars and *rishi munis* (seers) used to light fires and chant mantras for mental and emotional well-being. Those fires are called *hawans*[1] and they too had a scientific importance. Those fires were practised to fight neuro diseases. The vapours of the volatile oils used for a *yagna* had a way

---

[1] Hawan: https://www.thehindu.com/sci-tech/ancient-fire-ritual-has-positive-impact-on-environment-scientists/article2103881.ece

of entering the central nervous system via the nasal route and calming it.

Something as usual as wearing a bindi[2] on your forehead has a scientific backing. Pressing the point between your brows improves blood circulation, opens the nerves and regulates proper functioning of the central nervous system. It also helps you to enhance your concentration abilities.

Indian and Bohemian cultures boast of fabulous henna designs that also have another great purpose to serve besides aesthetic appeal. Mehndi is a great medicinal herb that can banish pre-wedding jitters. This medicinal herb has a cooling and calming effect on the body that keeps nerves from getting tense and fever from catching on. And that is not all—it is antiseptic and, of course, anti-inflammatory. So it shields the bride from negative energies with a legit justification.

Did you know that the echoing sound of the conch (*shankh*) can kill malaria mosquitoes and germs in the surroundings? Yes, there's a reason to leave your footwear outside before entering a temple.

The more you'll question why a certain activity or tradition is practised in a certain way, you'll have very logical answers to why our ancestors had our best interests in mind.

Roots to Radiance is so millennial, but the purpose of this book is also to respect tradition. Not necessarily

---

2   Bindi: https://en.wikipedia.org/wiki/Bindu_(symbol)

supporting orthodox beliefs or dogmatism—that's what most people get wrong about tradition.

By respecting tradition and rituals, this is my tribute to different practices—to respect the origins of these healing aids that don't get their due.

In this chapter, I would like to pick some useful ingredients from nature and help you incorporate them in your lives by making it as fun and easy as possible. Nature is calling out to you to make use of its many components.

These recipes will teach you how to treat your body beauty issues. Without hurting your pocket or leaving the house, there's so much you can work upon. From questioning the backing of traditions comes understanding, from understanding comes knowledge to put nature's offerings to good use, from using them comes the treatment of your concerns, and from being able to treat them comes empowerment and gratitude.

And when gratitude and empowerment is with you, nothing can defeat you. When you own up to your shortcomings and decide to work on them, it's the only approach you need to transform lives. Not just in terms of beauty—when 'roots to victory' becomes your way of life, you'll get the hang of applying basic formulas to solve complex situations. Let me say it again, I want this to be your way of life! So many ways to take control of your beauty routine with cruelty-free, sulphate/paraben- and toxin-free recipes, I really hope this book transforms your idea of beauty as it has for me.

Most of our health, skin and hair concerns are caused by an imbalance that occurs due to dryness in our veins. Keeping these oils on your bedside table and using over three drops in and around your belly button (navel) before sleeping can solve several problems. Your navel detects the veins that have dried up and unclogs them so that these oils reach them.

Neem oil treats acne, itching and rashes; almond oil enhances internal and external radiance; olive oil improves fertility, insomnia, constipation, liver functions and blood pressure; mustard oil boosts hair growth, hydrates dry/chapped lips; coconut oil prevents premature graying and dandruff; lemon oil improves pigmentation; pumpkin oil treats dry skin and cracked heels; castor oil helps promote lash growth; and grapeseed oil balances your navel.

1. Body Polishing and De-tanning

Tanning, sunburn, dull skin, ingrown hair—there's so much life and lifestyle will throw at you and your body. Little do the odds ever know that you're capable of fighting it all.

Pollution, physical/mental stress, questionable eating habits and sleep pattern—you need to give your body more credit than you usually do for sustaining you with so much grace. And when you've made it this far so gracefully, when you've not been so disciplined, imagine what you'd do if you added some healthy rules to your routine.

For instance, this amazing body scrub is a multitasker like you . . . it helps get rid of ingrown hair and eliminates dead skin and polishes your body. Using it twice a week will change the way your skin feels by giving it a silky smooth texture and lightening any scars.

SCRUB 1

½ cup watermelon juice
½ cup cucumber juice
½ cup tomato juice
¾ cup lemon juice
½ cup papaya juice
½ cup cucumber extract
½ cup carrot juice
½ cup red lentil (*masoor* dal)
½ cup rice
15 dried neem leaves
15 dried pink and white *desi gulab* petals
2 tablespoons powdered orange peel
2 tablespoons powdered lemon peel
2 tablespoons nutmeg (*jaifal*) powder

- Extract the juice of watermelon, cucumber, tomato, lemon, papaya and carrot and mix together.
- Soak the rice and red lentil in the juice mixture and leave it overnight. Next day, prepare to be amazed at how the rice and lentils have soaked in the juice.
- Let the juice-soaked rice and lentils dry in sunlight for a day or two.

- Once it's dried, mix it with dried neem leaves, lemon and orange peel powder (grind dried orange/lemon peel to make this), dried pink and white *desi gulab* petals and grated nutmeg (preferably 3).
- Then put all ingredients in a mixer grinder and grind to a fine powder.
- Your powder scrub is ready!

For oily skin: Mix the powdered scrub with curd and apply on your whole body. Let it dry for 10 mins and start taking it off like *ubtan*. Rinse your body with lukewarm water.

For normal/dry skin: Add cream (*malai*) and almond oil along with curd to the powdered scrub and follow the same procedure as above.

You can also use this as a face scrub by adding honey with the same ingredients. But scrub your face very, very gently.

SCRUB 2

½ cup cinnamon powder
1 cup dried blueberries
2 tablespoons brown sugar
¼ cup virgin coconut oil

Blueberries are packed with plenty of antioxidants and Vitamin C. Hence, they act as a rich moisturizer for your face as well as body. Cinnamon too has antioxidants and antibacterial properties that eliminate acne-causing bacteria. With the mix of these two, this moisturizing scrub mask can reduce redness and retain skin's hydration level.

- Dry the fresh blueberries and freeze them overnight.
- Next day, crush them and mix with cinnamon powder or ground cinnamon, brown sugar, and virgin coconut oil.
- Mix thoroughly and store in a jar.
- Use this moisturizing scrub mask to exfoliate and hydrate the skin on your face or body.

SCRUB 3

4–5 strawberries
2 tablespoons powdered lemon peel
2 tablespoons honey

This mask has brightening, exfoliating and anti-ageing goodness. Apart from Vitamin C and powerful exfoliation, this has antibacterial and smoothening ingredients—honey.

Blend the strawberries and add lemon peel powder and honey to it. Mix well and apply to body to remove unwanted impurities, dirt, germs—and smell amazing!

2. Ubtans

Haldi ubtan is applied to the bride's body before the wedding for an unmatched glow. Apart from anti-inflammatory, antiseptic properties found in turmeric, the other elements of *ubtan* help calm the body, release stress, detoxify the skin cells and get the body ready for the bride to go through all the never-ending celebrations.

In this section, I am covering a few very efficient *ubtan*s that are a must in a busy girl's life, whether she is a to-be-bride or not. Stress is a factor in everyone's life. And there's nothing like a good old body-energizing, sense-calming *ubtan* every once in a while to reverse the damages of a busy and stressful environment.

a. Ubtan 1

1 peeled cucumber
7–8 slices of peeled papaya
7 full tablespoons chickpea flour
1 teaspoon turmeric
Juice of 1 lemon
2–3 slice of bread
10 drops of almond oil
1 full cup cream

- Grind cucumber and papaya.
- Add chickpea flour, turmeric, lemon juice, *malai*, and almond oil to it.
- Mix well and add the slices of bread and mix it with your hands. Make sure this mixture isn't too liquidy. In fact, it should be thick.
- Apply this *ubtan* to full arms, legs, chest, belly and back and wait for 10–12 minutes.
- When the *ubtan* begins to dry, start removing it by rubbing it to and fro, section by section of the whole body, till it has fully rolled off your skin.

Yeast found in bread is an antioxidant that helps reduce redness and irritation. It smoothens the texture of your body like nothing else and contributes majorly to the regeneration of new skin cells. And the other ingredients of the *ubtan* soothe, smoothen, and add a glow and radiance to the texture of your skin. This *ubtan* will make your skin feel smoother than ever for a good full week.

b. Ubtan 2

2 tablespoons powdered orange peel
2 tablespoons powdered lemon peel
2 tablespoons nutmeg powder
2 tablespoons sandalwood powder
2 tablespoons red lentil powder
A little less than 1 cup milk cream
1 teaspoon turmeric
2 teaspoons saffron

The quality and texture of this *ubtan* also needs to be thick and a little coarse.

- Mix powdered lemon peel, orange peel, nutmeg, sandalwood, red lentil and turmeric with cream and saffron.
- Add coconut oil just enough to mix the ingredients well.
- Apply this to your full body and leave it for 10 minutes.
- After 10 minutes, start removing it by rubbing it back and forth, section by section of your whole body till it's fully rolled off your skin.

This *ubtan* has very easily available ingredients. This will not only help brighten and refresh your skin but also help lighten scars. Without leaving the house or buying anything extra, this *ubtan* is a fabulous way for all skin types to detoxify and hit the reboot button for your body on weekends.

3. Stretch Marks and Cellulite

Whether you've had a baby, lost a lot of weight or just find no legit reasons to have stretch marks but you have them, don't worry, you're not alone. Every girl has them in some area or the other. One artist from Barcelona, Cinta Tort Cartró, even went #InstaFamous for rendering the cellulite marks with glitter paints to make art. And let's agree how amazing the digital world is to give us the courage to own up to what we are and motivate us to help us become what we want to become. We are so lucky to be alive in times when there's acceptance for every emotion, thought and habit that we may have. The Internet is often hated for its toxicity. People either OD on it or go for a social media detox . . . like working in extremes is any healthy.

No one talks about striking a balance where we manage how much to indulge in something and how to restrict ourselves. And no matter how many times you fail to meet your set standards, eventually getting to a point of balance will always benefit you far better than living in extremes.

In a way, I would like to relate that to cellulite and stretch marks. It is something that we can manage and control, and if we put in just the right amount of effort, we can control it if not fade its existence altogether.

Light or intense, improving stretch marks/cellulite with natural remedy is not that hard. Applying coconut oil immediately after a hot bath and brushing the areas that have cellulite stimulates your body's lymphatic system. Another technique is 'dry brushing'.

Let alone cellulite, dry brushing is the best way to cleanse, detox, unclog pores, and exfoliate your body. To complete this method, all you'll need is a firm yet soft bristled body brush.

After you take a bath, pat your body dry and slather coconut oil all over you body and start massaging it with a brush from toe towards your chest area. Be gentle and massage in circular motion from bottom to the top. Since you're massaging an oil into your body with this brush, make extra efforts to keep your brush clean as an oily brush will attract dirt and bacteria faster . . . this is one of the non-traditional methods to shoo off those marks.

Here are some DIY masks, oils and mixtures to help these marks lighten over time.

Cellulite-Fading Coffee Mask 1

½ cup coffee powder (coffee grounds)
¼ cup coconut oil
½ cup white sugar crystals

This is a very simple mask but highly effective. Coconut oil alone reduces the appearance of stretch marks and cellulite. Caffeine has antioxidants and has an ability to dilate blood vessels and tighten skin.

- Mix coffee grounds, coconut oil and sugar to form a thick paste.
- Apply to the parts of the body that may have cellulite, like your lower belly, bikini line, breasts, butt, etc., and massage gently.
- Leave on for 10–15 minutes and rinse with lukewarm water.
- Repeat every alternate day if you can to reduce the appearance of those marks over time.

Stretch Marks Banishing Oil-In-Mask 2

3 green tea bags
4 tablespoons crushed chia seeds
2 tablespoons grapefruit oil (optional)
2 tablespoons lemongrass oil
2 tablespoons rosemary oil

Chia seeds have antioxidants and vitamins that help tone the body. Grapefruit, lemongrass and rosemary oils are the kings of cellulite-reducing oils. This mask is sure going to smell delicious and effective!

- Dip the tea bags in hot water and take them out.
- Cut up the bags and take out the freshly soaked leaves.
- Add the oils and chia seeds to those leaves and mix well.
- Apply the mask to the areas where you have stretch marks.

- Repeat twice or thrice a week to lighten the appearance of those marks.
- You can minus the chia seeds and green tea leaves and can apply these oils individually to affected areas for when you're too busy.

Stretch Marks Banishing Gentle Mask 3

½ cup aloe vera extract
¼ cup cucumber juice
¼ cup lemon juice
3 apricots
1 tablespoon nutmeg powder
2 tablespoon almond oil
A few drops of juniper oil (optional)

Aloe vera makes skin heal and regenerate new cells. Cucumber, lemon and nutmeg help reduce the appearance of scars and marks. Almond oil hydrates the skin and apricots have rejuvenational tendencies.

- Deseed the apricots and grind them to make a paste.
- Add cucumber juice, lemon juice, aloe vera extract, nutmeg powder and almond oil.
- Make a paste and apply to affected area.
- Repeat thrice, weekly.

Juniper oil decreases fluid retention and relaxes tissues that further helps eliminate cellulite. Using this oil alone can do the job well in this case, but if it isn't available, you can totally skip using it in the recipe.

Stretch Marks Eliminating Body Balm 4

¼ cup coconut oil
2 tablespoons beeswax
3 tablespoons grapefruit oil/juniper oil/lemongrass oil/rosemary oil
2 tablespoons apple cider vinegar
8–10 drops of lemon oil

How can I let you break your cellulite-fighting routine if you are a girl who's always on the move?

In this fight to fade stretch marks, you can carry this body balm even when you're travelling, to make sure your skincare routine doesn't suffer.

- Melt coconut and beeswax together, mix well and keep aside.
- In another pan, mix apple cider vinegar, lemon essential oil and grapefruit oil (or juniper/rosemary/lemongrass oil, or a few drops of all if you have them, but not more than 20 drops in total).
- Heat the pan till the oils blend fully.
- Then mix it with previously heated mixture of beeswax and coconut oil.
- Mix all ingredients together and pour into a jar you wish to store this balm in.
- Apply twice a day.

Post Pregnancy Easy-to-Make Belly Oil 5

New mom? You've got enough on your plate. What most moms complain about post their pregnancy is that they didn't have enough time to take care of their 'mom bod'. Enters this two-ingredient belly oil that'll help fade the stretch marks as fast as it gets. It's best to start using this oil and incorporate it into your routine from your fifth or sixth month. Now I know I haven't birthed children, but my mom lost around 15 kilos and went back to her original weight after a couple of months when I was born, and this oil was her fastest method to fade stretch marks.

½ cup aloe vera extract
½ cup virgin coconut oil

Mix these two ingredients together and apply on your belly daily to reduce the appearance of stretch marks.

4. *Managing Sagging Skin*

Toning your body and treating sagging skin is a part of age reversal. Defying age is one of the constant battles one deals with after reaching a certain age. But the best approach to look at this is to stop fighting and start managing. Getting your skin concerns in control without obsessing too hard is one good, steady method to reaching skin goals over time.

There are a lot of factors that contribute to skin sagging. Smoking, junk food, reduction in production of collagen, and the obvious one—ageing.

Here are a few DIY ideas to manage loose and sagging skin:

Skin Firming Body Water 1

Water
Potassium alum (*fitkari*)

Let me back this up with the most street-smart technique that's spotted in the tents of local barbers in our country. They keep blocks of *fitkari* with them and use it as an aftershave balm. Reason being, it's antiseptic, it shrinks open pores and also helps repair loose skin.

- Just add 2 blocks of potassium alum to a bucketful of water and let it dissolve.
- Bathe in that water to tighten your skin.
- You can also use half a cup for one cup of water and dissolve it to apply to the areas that have stretch marks, as a skin-tightening mask.

Skin Firming Aloe Oatmeal Mask 2

1 cup aloe vera gel
¼ cup coconut milk
3 tablespoons ground oatmeal
2 tablespoons bentonite clay

2 tablespoons cornstarch
10 drops grapefruit oil

The significance of aloe vera, ground ointments (or non-instant oatmeal powder), grapefruit oil and other starches in terms of firming are explained in this book. This mask brings together the best of all firming ingredients in one recipe.

- Mix aloe vera gel or extracts with oatmeal, bentonite clay, cornstarch, grapefruit oil and coconut milk.
- Mix well and apply to your skin twice or thrice a week for 20 minutes before bathing.
- This will keep your skin firm and youthful.

Rajma Rice Body Toning and Depigmenting Mask 3

4–5 tablespoons powdered kidney beans
3 tablespoons powdered rice
¼ cup potato juice

Bagging some packs of rajma and rice at the grocery store for your lunches and dinners? Well, pack a few grams more, as we've come to making the most budget-friendly mask ever. Move over, not leaving your house to fix skin concerns, for this mask you probably won't have to move from one corner of your kitchen to another, because all of these three ingredients are probably kept together.

Potato, kidney beans and rice, sounds like lunch to me! But kidney beans are insanely high on proteins and hence help tone and firm the body. Rice does the same, it tightens skin, regulates blood circulation and boosts cell renewal. Potato juice works on uneven skin tone and fights pigmentation.

- Put a handful of kidney beans and rice in the blender to powder it.
- Stir in the potato juice and mix well.
- Apply on your full body to make it toned, radiant and even.
- Use this mask on your body at least thrice a week to achieve best results.
- You can even add a few drops of lavender oil, if you want to.

Butt and Breasts Firming Mask 4

7 tablespoons powdered barley
2 tablespoons extra virgin coconut oil
2 tablespoons extra virgin olive oil
½ cup egg whites
2 teaspoons honey

I've used the king of cereals—barley—for this one! It fights fine lines, loose and wrinkled skin.

People complain about sagging breasts more often than they talk about flat, sagging butts. One of the obvious reasons for it is because we get to see our frontal more often in the mirror than our back. And when we take out that bikini on a vacation is when the appearance of our butt comes to our attention. Don't know about you, but it happens to me all the time.

Sagging breasts are so common after pregnancy or drastic weight loss. Your skin loses a lot of fat, making them sag, and that sagging is reversed by this mask.

- Blend a full cup of barley to make a powder out of it.
- Add extra virgin coconut oil, olive oil, egg white and honey to it and mix well.
- Apply to areas that you need to firm and leave it on for 30 minutes and rinse.

Pomegranate and Blackthorn Calf and Bikini Lines Firming/Stretch Marks Fading Mask 5

½ cup pomegranate juice
3–4 tablespoons kaolin clay
2 tablespoons blackthorn oil

The antioxidants in pomegranate juice replenish the skin and chase wrinkles away. Blackthorn oil is an unusual oil that tones the skin in miraculous ways. Don't mistake it for buckthorn oil while buying it online, though. But if you do end up buying buckthorn by mistake, I've placed it in another body wash recipe for you.

Kaolin clay (chini mitti) unclogs pores and make skin supple and even, in terms of texture.

- Add pomegranate juice to kaolin clay and blackthorn oil.
- Mix well to make a paste and apply it to your bikini lines, calves or wherever you wish to shoo away loose skin and stretch marks.
- Leave on for 20–30 minutes and rinse.

Multi-Purpose Body-Firming and Hydrating Body Lotion 6

4 tablespoons shea butter
3 tablespoons beeswax
1 tablespoon almond oil
1 tablespoon sandalwood oil
1 tablespoon juniper oil (optional but an amazing ingredient to tighten skin)
1 tablespoon marula oil (optional but an amazing ingredient to tighten skin)
1 teaspoon jasmine essential oil

- Melt the shea butter and beeswax in a pan in medium heat.
- Then add almond and all the other oils in that order and mix well.
- The cream is ready.
- Put it in a jar, let it cool down and close the lid.

You can start using this DIY skin-firming and soothing cream that'll not only moisturize your skin, but also smell great. Marula and juniper oil are optional, but they're super effective when it comes to cell renewal and wrinkle-fighting situations.

5. Body Oils

Let's admit it, hydrating your skin is never a bad idea. Applying cream, oils or serums, feeding your skin with essential nutrients, vitamins, antioxidants, anti-ageing components and other rejuvenating oils will only be the smartest way to be prepared for the changes your body will go through. Here are some DIY oil recipes for all skin conditions.

Body Brightening Night Oil 1

¼ cup argan oil
2 teaspoon rose oil
1 teaspoon lavender oil
½ teaspoon lemon oil
½ teaspoon sandalwood oil
½ teaspoon carrot seed oil
½ teaspoon chamomile oil

I have shared with you previously recipes for the rose lip balm and hand cream that you can use, so how could I miss a body oil to match?

If you have essential oils ready, this skin-brightening oil will be child's play for you.

- Argan oil is the carrier oil in this recipe. Pour that into a miniature bottle first, even before you start adding essential oils.
- After you have poured argan oil, add the other oils in that order.
- Apply to your skin and say goodbye to dryness.

This oil removes dark spots too, so prepare to welcome fresh, glowing skin. Apply to your skin only once at night to wake up smelling like a flower.

This is best used as post-shower night oil.

Skin Tightening Oil 2

¼ cup castor oil
2 teaspoons rosehip oil
1 teaspoon neroli oil
1 teaspoon primrose oil

This oil mixture is very niche. Castor oil is the carrier oil in this recipe. If you own a full set of essential oils, which I insist you do, just pour castor oil in a bottle and add the other essential oils in that order.

Shake well and apply to your body to tighten your skin and defy signs of ageing.

Oil-in-Sunscreen 3

½ cup olive oil
15 basil leaves
¼ cup beeswax
2 tablespoons shea butter
¼ cup coconut oil
1 teaspoon carrot seed oil

- Heat the olive oil. Add the basil leaves to it and stir gently.

- After 15–20 minutes, filter the oil and separate it from the leaves.
- Now you have a heated, basil-infused olive oil as a base.
- Add the beeswax and stir till it dilutes properly.
- Then add the coconut oil, shea butter and carrot seed oil.
- Store it in a jar and close the lid after you are done.

Shea butter and coconut oil have natural SPF-5, and beeswax is also considered a great sun resistant. Carrot juice fights sun damage and so does the carrot seed oil, as used in this recipe. This is an inexpensive, everyday sunscreen that'll fight sun damage even when you're not leaving the house.

6. Discoloured Underarms, Elbows, Knees and Uneven Skin Tone

Dryness, excess exposure to sun and ignoring certain parts of the body while caring for the rest can leave a drastic difference in the colour of the skin in the same area. I'm talking about the colour of your arms being drastically different from the elbows and underarms. And the colour of your thighs being quite brighter than your knees. Relax! It's in skin's nature to change shades from part to part.

Here we are going to make certain masks that will even your skin tone, whether it's light or dark. This is not a lightening treatment—just an attempt to make your skin tone look even, whatever the shade of your skin may be.

Underarms Clearing Mask 1

¼ cup aloe vera extract
2 teaspoons apple cider vinegar
2 teaspoons baking soda

These are all cleansing and sunburn fighting ingredients.

- Add all ingredients together to make a thick paste.
- Apply to underarms thrice a week to fight discolouration.
- Try to lift your arms and keep that area airy as much as possible to avoid discolouration.

Supple Elbows and Knees Mask 2

1 tablespoon Fuller's earth clay
1 tablespoon raw milk
1 teaspoon turmeric powder
1 teaspoon honey (optional)
1 tablespoon lemon juice
1 tablespoon tomato juice

Fresh lemon peel alone is a good go-to when it comes to practising natural methods for supple skin. But this mask will give it the proper moisturization and clearing agents that your skin needs.

- Mix Fuller's earth clay with raw milk, honey, turmeric, lemon and tomato juice.
- Make a paste and use it as an elbow-knee clearing mask, thrice a week to flaunt even-toned legs.
- Do follow up with coconut oil after the mask is removed/rinsed.

MASK 3

¼ cup potato juice
4 drops of tea tree oil
A few drops of marula oil (optional)

- Add a few drops of tea tree oil to potato juice and apply to dark knees and elbows.
- Apply thrice a week and follow up with a moisturizer after the mask is removed.

As explained before, potato juice fights hyperpigmentation like a pro. And tea tree has antibacterial, spot-clearing properties. Marula oil brightens and boosts cell renewal.

7. DIY Body Washes

Body washes, the most basic everyday need! What if I told you—you can not only sort these by flavour but also get to separate it by skin quality—dry, oily, sensitive and so on. Let's get you to make your own body washes that'll rock your world and give you the morning boost you need to stay motivated all day.

Calming Moringa Mint Body Wash 1

½ cup liquid castile soap
2 tablespoons coconut oil
2 tablespoons glycerine
4 tablespoons spearmint or peppermint oil
3 tablespoons lavender oil
2 tablespoons moringa oil
1 teaspoon hemp oil (optional)

This body wash is safe for people who have sensitive and acne-prone skin. Hemp oil is great for skin that suffers from rosacea and frequent redness. Moringa, lavender and peppermint/spearmint are all cooling agents that'll pamper your skin while you take a bath.

- Mix all ingredients in a cup, in the same order, and store in a pump bottle. Your daily body wash is ready.

Honey Chamomile Hydrating Body Wash 2

½ cup liquid castile soap
½ cup raw honey
3 tablespoons chamomile oil
2 tablespoons Vitamin E oil

If you have dull and dry skin, change that with the goodness of honey and chamomile present in this body wash recipe. This body wash cleanses body without making it dry.

- Mix all ingredients in a cup, in the same order, and store in a pump bottle.

Excess Oil Removing Tea Tree Eucalyptus Body Wash 3

½ cup original coconut milk
½ cup liquid castile soap
2 tablespoons jojoba oil
2 teaspoons glycerine
2 teaspoon drops tea tree essential oil
1 teaspoon eucalyptus oil

If you have oily skin, you can remove excess oils and dirt by the effects of eucalyptus and tea tree oils in this recipe.

- Mix the coconut milk and castile soap, then add the other ingredients and mix well.
- Store in a pump bottle and use regularly.

8. DIY Loofah

When giving away body wash recipes, one can't not think of adding a natural loofah. I have such a faint memory of my mom filling a bucket with heated water and adding shampoo and almond oil to it. And the loofah was unbelievable when I used to watch the level of cleaning and exfoliating it did.

All you need to get a natural bath sponge/loofah is dried ridge gourd. Yes, our good old *turai*. This vegetable still hangs strong in its tree even when it's dried. All you have to do is pluck it and remove the peel, and your loofah is ready. The dried ridge is your bathing sponge! Just dip it in hot water for half an hour to make sure it becomes soft before use. And then start using it every day with your body wash to exfoliate your skin while bathing with the most natural ingredients.

> Don't love yourself for your potential . . . that's in future. Love yourself for what you are now and today. While having a vision for your upcoming self is great, your body, soul, and heart need love and appreciation today, starting now!

7

Hands and Feet

By the power vested in you by the universe, have the courage to take big steps without doubting yourself. Have a firm hand when it comes to your beliefs, and put your foot down not just to make a point but also to flaunt how gorgeous they are.

Try not to freak out when I tell you this, but hands are the #1 body part that shows signs of ageing.

Here's a short horror story: While you're busy keeping your face flawless, and your hair luscious, your hands felt ignored, they aged, and suddenly there's not much you can do about it.

Moral: Better safe than sorry!

There's a reason why Grace Kelly[1] was strict and particular about keeping her hands hydrated and moisturized, says

---

[1] https://www.byrdie.com/grace-kelly-beauty-secrets

beauty expert Peter Lamas, who's worked with her on many projects. 'When I asked her why, she replied, "A woman's age shows on her hand much quicker than anywhere else",' he added.

But wait, she wasn't the only royal who was obsessed with keeping her hands beautiful. Queen Victoria also has something in common with her. She was said to perfume her hand gloves with rose oil. Now that's one way to make your handshake more memorable.

Your struggle to keep your hands looking beautiful doesn't end at getting rid of the leftover dyes when you remove a dark nail polish, but also at making nails look shiny even when you have no nail paints on.

The trick is to add a DIY TLC for your hands and feet to your bi-weekly routine that'll help you defy ageing in the long run. And the benefits of hand and feet care are not just restricted to superficial beauty; this procedure can even help you relax, improve your blood circulation, not to mention that it's also got the hygiene part of the equation covered.

When you were a child you were instructed by your elders to keep your nails clean. They even tried to scare you by saying that having long nails could poison your food.

And under their supervision, you followed those rules until you became a grown-up, and began to care about health a lot less and about style a lot more. Which is when nail extensions came into the picture.

Your hands and feet collect the maximum dirt from your surroundings.

That also makes it clear that they are the most active and busy parts of your body. So, now would be time the time to stop neglecting them. You even end up touching your face very often with those very hands.

Start with moisturizing your cuticles regularly, scrubbing your hands regularly and applying sunscreen on them every single day. Here are some ways to make your own scrubs, salves and oils that are fit for the fabulous treatments your hands and feet deserve.

Do wash your hands and feet and clean the nail areas with a baby toothbrush before applying these oils, masks and scrubs.

1. Hand and Foot Scrubs

SCRUB 1: Sea Salt + Sugar + Glycerine

Sea salt alone is an efficient enough scrub, but adding a few drops of almond oil, white or brown sugar with glycerine and lemon makes for a wholesome remedy for hydrating rough, dull hand skin.

- Mix 4 tablespoons sea salt, 3 teaspoons glycerine and 2 teaspoons sugar together with a few drops of almond oil and lemon juice.
- Apply this mixture to the upper and inner parts of your hands, basically your full hands.
- Don't forget to spread a paper sheet or piece of cloth underneath your hands/feet to avoid a mess.

- Rub your hands together and massage feet gently for 8–10 minutes.
- Wash off and apply hand cream.

SCRUB 2: Rose Water + Baking Soda + Vitamin E Capsule

Baking soda is a very capable cleaner and Vitamin E brings glow and moisturization. Rose water combines these two beautifully. This mask can help remove tan, dirt and dead skin in no time, leaving your hands/feet feeling softer than ever. Mix 3 tablespoons baking soda with 2 tablespoons rosewater and cut open 2 Vitamin E capsules and add the extracts to the mixture. Mix well and scrub away for glowy, smooth hands and feet.

SCRUB 3: Epsom Salt + Olive Oil + Peppermint Oil

Bathing with Epsom salt water can even help you lose weight[2]. Peppermint oil will freshen your senses. And olive oil will help with dry feet and hands.

- Mix 3 tablespoons Epsom salt with 1 tablespoon olive oil and 10–12 drops of peppermint oil.
- Mix well and apply to hands and feet for a multitasking scrub session.

---

[2] https://www.femniqe.com/epsom-salt-weight-loss/
https://www.emaxhealth.com/8782/10-minute-trick-get-you-your-skinny-jeans-party
https://www.healthambition.com/epsom-salt-bath-weight-loss-benefits/

2. Cracked Heels

If only wearing socks regularly saved us from cracked heels, skincare routine could have cut down one thing, *just one thing*, from the list. But no, sock fabric had to suck moisture out of our skin, leaving it dry and cracked.

While you take out weekends to do your own mani-pedi by these methods, here's something to help you heal your heels!

a. The P3 Mask

2–3 slices of papaya
2–3 slices of pineapple
2–3 slices of pumpkin
2 tablespoons honey

I'm calling this a P3 mask because it combines the goodness of pineapple, papaya and pumpkin . . . all excellent skin-healing components combined with the smoothing maestro—honey!

- Scrub your feet and apply this smoothie.

b. Mint–Chickpea Healing Mask

½ cup boiled rice water
2½ tablespoons chickpea or gram flour
1 tablespoon peppermint oil

When making rice, do save some of the starch water instead of throwing it away. It has supreme reviving powers for your skin (and fabrics). This mask has bonding and reviving capabilities.

- Mix that starch water with gram/chickpea flour and add peppermint oil.
- Scrub your foot and apply it.
- Follow up by applying shea butter or any foot creams/oils mentioned below.

3. Hand + Nail Salves

Nails and hands should never be neglected in your beauty regime as they age first. But if you think I'm being strict with you, let me just tell you that just like most chapters, this one will also teach you how to customize your own kind of hand and foot lotions, so that your salves/lotions can change with your mood for the day.

a. Cedar Wood–Neroli Hand Salve

¼ cup original shea butter
1½ tablespoon beeswax
4 tablespoons jojoba oil (can be replaced with almond, olive or any good carrier oil of your choice)
1 tablespoon cedar wood oil
1 teaspoon neroli oil

- Melt beeswax, shea butter and coconut oil and let it cool down for 20 mins.
- Then add jojoba, cedar wood and neroli oil and stir well.
- Store it in a jar and use as a hand soother.

Trust me, it'll smell unbelievably delicious and earthy, like you've entered one of those luxurious Ayurveda spas.

You can switch cedar wood oil with rose oil and neroli oil with sandalwood oil and make a rose–sandalwood hand salve—that's not a bad idea either. In fact, just try it! That makes this count as two recipes!

b. Green Tea–Jasmine Hand Cream

¼ cup original shea butter
1½ tablespoons beeswax
½ cup coconut oil
2 green tea bags (fresh/unused)
2 tablespoons jasmine essential oil

- Simmer the green tea leaves in coconut oil in a pan and stir well.
- Then separate the green tea leaves from the coconut oil and keep it aside.
- Take another pan and melt beeswax and mix shea butter with it and let it cool for 20 mins.
- Then add the green tea-infused coconut oil and jasmine oil to it.

- Mix everything well—and your hand cream is ready!

4. Cuticle Oils

Cuticles, the delicate skin located at the edge of your fingers and toes, are something even most particular beauty enthusiasts don't care much for. But you should! This skin protects your new growth from infections and bacteria, and if we're talking beautiful hands and feet, this is a procedure you shouldn't skip, especially if you colour your nails or wear extensions. Nail paints and extensions dehydrate your nails and keep them from generating new nail cells.

If you are experiencing frequent peeling, redness, itchiness and discoloration, maybe it's time to moisturize your cuticles super well before you apply nail paint again.

Here are a few DIY cuticle oil recipes that you can use for different purposes:

a. Nourishing Cuticle Oil

3 teaspoons argan oil
3 teaspoons castor oil
2 teaspoons avocado oil
2 teaspoons grapeseed oil

Argan oil will make up for lost moisture around your nails. Avocado oil can moisturize your skin and leave it smoother than ever. Castor oil has antifungal, antibacterial properties, and grapeseed oil is a comparatively lighter oil that has vitamins C, D and E.

- Mix these oils together and apply on the nail beds of your fingers and toes using an earbud to eliminate itchy and dry cuticles.

b. Coconut, Lavender and Honey Cuticle Salve

¼ cup coconut oil
1½ tablespoons beeswax
2 tablespoons honey
2 teaspoons lavender oil

- Melt beeswax and coconut oil in a saucepan and add honey and lavender oil.
- Mix well and let it cool down.
- Then pour it in a jar and let it solidify.

This salve will be like a lip balm, but for your nails. It's hugely hydrating and efficient on your mission to get clean, soft hands and feet.

5. Nail-Strengthening

The primary reason people go for nail extensions is because their nails keep breaking. But what happens after you take off your nail extensions is even more alarming! Your nails become so weak after you take your acrylics off. Hence, people resort to it again and again till they eventually give up and have weak nails for a while, repair them and then get back to having shiny, original nails over time.

Nail Growth Boosting Tea

This is just nettle tea with a much-needed kick of Vitamin C! Nettle leaves (*bichhoo ghaans*) boost nail growth, and Vitamin C guards your nails by strengthening your blood vessels, skin, tissues and cuticles.

- Boil 1 tablespoon nettle leaves in one cup water and then filter out the leaves once the tea is ready.
- Add the juice of ½ lemon in it and sip once a day to promote nail growth.

But the benefits are not just limited to your nails. This tea is a great hangover remedy and acts as a blood purifier too!

6. Nail Whitening and Cleansing

You would have ditched wearing nail paints in everyday life long ago if your original nails were shiny, shapely and even. Wearing chemicals on your nails leave them yellow and pigmented. They not only challenge the growth, colour and texture of your nails but they are also a threat to your hygiene.

Here are a few ways to cleanse and whiten your nails:

a. Whitening Paste

Any teeth whitening paste
A few drops of lemon juice
½ teaspoon baking soda

- Mix these three ingredients together and you can whiten teeth and yellow nails with it!

Bid farewell to stains left by your nail paints and extensions by using this easy method.

And start applying a protecting/nail strengthening base coat before applying pigments directly on to your nails.

b. Nail Depigmenting Gel

⅛ cup aloe vera extract/gel
3 teaspoons tea tree oil
3 teaspoons garlic oil

Aloe vera will form a soothing layer on your nails to prevent irritation while tea tree and ginger oil fights the fungus in your hand and toe nails.

- Mix the three ingredients together and apply a thin layer on your nails whenever possible.

8

Oral Hygiene

When I've written a full book on becoming a #CleanBeauty convert, and put a healthy smile on your face, I'll have to make sure your pearly whites look great too! Bad breath, stained teeth or anything remotely close to bad hygiene is such a turn off. On the other hand, if someone is hygiene-conscious and cares about wearing the right perfume, having fresh breath and tidy nails, they're instantly attractive.

If you have to schedule a consultation with a dentist, a dermatologist and a gynaecologist, which one are you likely to place at the last? The answer usually is the dentist!

Most dental treatments are painful and end up with you heading home with a swollen mouth and the prospect of pain while eating for the next few days. And your favourite foods and desserts are already not a part of the question for the next few weeks. Just these few weeks of compromise and sacrifice can demotivate you to see a dentist for ages, and the next thing you know, you're 40 and having serious dental issues.

Many of us do take dental health casually, even though we should not.

In other chapters I've explained how to get rid of nearly every possible beauty issue. Teeth and dental hygiene spills over to wellness more than beauty, but these easy everyday hacks had to be talked about. Routine dental check-ups are a must and taking care of your mouth by yourself is a non-negotiable.

Teeth Whitening Paste 1

1 tablespoon coconut oil
1 teaspoon turmeric
2 teaspoons baking soda

Although I have a quick hack to brighten teeth in my Under Three Minutes Hacks section, here's another one.

- Mix baking soda, turmeric and coconut oil together and brush normally. No, your teeth will not be pigmented by the colour of turmeric—don't worry about that.
- Rinse mouth with water normally after you're done.

Teeth Whitening Paste 2

1 tablespoon coconut oil
1 teaspoon baking soda

2 teaspoons activated charcoal
3 drops of eucalyptus oil or spearmint oil

- Mix baking soda, activated charcoal, coconut oil and spearmint/eucalyptus oil together and brush normally.
- Rinse mouth normally with water after you're done.

Plaque Eliminating Solution 3

Plaque is a very common dental problem. Swollen gums, bad breath, stained teeth are a few of its symptoms. Here's how you can keep all these problems away.

1 cup water
4 drops of tea tree oil

- Just dilute tea tree oil and water together and use it like a mouthwash. This antibacterial is a strong weapon when it comes to keeping your teeth and gums safe.
- Use twice every day.

Swollen Gums Treatment 4

1 teaspoon powdered clove
1 cup water
Cotton earbuds or cotton balls

Swollen gums happen when oral care doesn't exactly top your priority list.

Don't worry, here's how you can treat soothe your gums at home without freaking out.

- Boil water, add the clove powder and mix well.
- When the solution cools down, apply it to your gums to build a protective shield around them.

Guava Leaf Microbial Shield Water 5

20 guava leaves
1 cup water
Mortar and pestle

> Guava leaves have antibacterial, microbial properties. They act as an amazing shield to protect your mouth from germs and dental diseases.

- Crush guava leaves in the mortar and pestle and strain the juice properly.
- Add boiled water and filter the mixture to take all the dregs out.
- Gargle with that water every day.

Part II Tips and Hacks

9

Body Mists

Coco Chanel may have said that women who didn't wear perfume had no future, but that was decades ago. Over the past few years, we have been headed towards a more understated way of living—a more low-key way of life, where experiences, Internet, friends and modern philosophy have taught us to worry, dress, behave and be less and less bothered about pleasing anyone but ourselves. Suddenly the chase for stuff like dousing yourself with copious amounts of perfume to announce your persona when you enter a room and prove a point to seek approval from outside has faded.

Recently, I read somewhere that 'young people are the new old people'. And it brought a grin to my face, and I was like, us being 'too set in our ways' has finally paid off. The world thinks of us millennials as wise individuals who have a lot of clarity simply because we cut down on anything that seems unnecessary and make room for what feeds our soul.

On weekends, don't you just want to be at home with your special one and look, feel and be amazing? That's clarity.

Using free time to better ourselves and rewarding self with lighting some candles, drawing ourselves a scented bath and reading favourite books is a terrific idea—if that's what works for you, of course.

This chapter is written to celebrate the lady in you. We may be a meme-loving, social media-hooked generation, but let's admit it, we do love some old-fashioned stuff, from time to time.

'Sometimes I can't figure out whether you're a millennial or a Victorian,' an older friend of mine said to me when he found out about my obsession for teas and fancy kettles.

So while you think about that one hobby or habit of yours that makes you an old soul, gear up for making organic ingredients a thing of luxury in the most ladylike fashion.

In this chapter, I'll be talking about something I'd like to call 'body waters'. This may have made you think about body and face mists, right? Body waters are somewhat like that, but they are not packed in a bottle and you don't have to preserve them for months in your refrigerator. You just have to have those long bath therapy sessions with these scented waters. But then, this is going to be devoid of any harmful ingredients as you'll be making it yourself. What's even better? They're so easy—a child can do it.

Hardly any ingredients are involved in this procedure, these scented waters can change the way you feel and function. Washing toxins away and enhancing skin health may be the commonly known benefits of bathing early morning, but did you know you can improve fertility, banish stress and improve blood circulation if only you say yes to a morning bath during the weekends. And as you have the luxury of spending hours in the bathroom, you must do it in the most organic and healthy way.

1. Rose/Desi Gulab

When you put *desi gulab* petals in hot water, it makes the solution a rich mixture of Vitamin C, malic acid, pectin and citric acid that can also help you lose weight. But roses are as good for your outside as for your inside.

- Collect petals of 4–5 roses in a nylon mesh bag and dip it in water overnight.
- Add some drops of rose water in it.
- Next morning, take out the bag and bathe with that water.

Trust me it's the TLC your body needs. Having a therapeutic baths like this can turn your day around. Imagine smelling great without spraying any product on you. Just scented body mixed with your natural smell would put you in a great mood.

2. Lemongrass

If you ask an expert, they'll associate lemongrass with terms such as anti-inflammatory, anti-depressant, disinfectant, sedative and deodorant, etc., . . . which are just some of the amazing health benefits this plant carries.

The strong smell of lemongrass itself makes you feel like you're in a spa, and how would you feel about getting one every other day?

- All you need to do is dip lemongrass leaves (in a nylon mesh bag) in water and leave overnight.
- You can also add lemongrass oil to make your bathroom smell great too.
- Next day when you bathe in it, it'll not only deodorize your body, but also calm your head in the process.

This herb can even heal period cramps, muscle pulls and headaches. After a long day of work, try bathing in lemongrass water to see the difference.

3. Rosemary and Sandalwood

Rosemary is an antioxidant-rich herb that helps fight cancer and brain ageing. Not only that, it also smells delicious and is used to flavour food as well. And sandalwood is more than just a great-smelling log. It has properties to help with spasms, anxiety, check germs and is an anti-inflammatory like most ingredients in this list. Not just that, the oil of this wood also helps keep blood pressure in check. And what happens when you leave these two in a mesh bag overnight in a bucket? Well, nothing short of a magic body water for you to take a bath in. You can use these ingredients separately also. Depends on your mood.

4. *Lavender*

The ultimate night bath or lazy afternoon bathing solution. Wanna nap like a queen? Try this! Since ages, lavender has been the ultimate solution to stress and anxiety. Keeping lavender leaves in your pillow is said to help you get a good night's sleep.

- So what you need to do here is dip a small branch of lavender in a bucket for 7–8 hours and then bathe in it.

Not only will this make you and your bathroom smell delicious, it'll also help you fall asleep, relax and unwind.

5. *Mogra*

Such an intense smell if you just grab and smell this flower. But you can enjoy a faint, understated version of it that will be easy on your head and will keep you energized all day long.

- Zip 10–12 of these little flowers in a mesh bag and leave overnight, and bathe in it next morning.

You won't even rely on any other mist after using this one. Imagine smelling like this flower all day long—prepare for a lot of compliments from anybody you talk to or hug during the day!

10

Hacks by the Season

Just when you've figured out a way to retain good health despite pollution, stress and the outcome of your eating and sleeping pattern—the weather changed! And without an ounce of guilt, it demanded you to change your creams, your shampoo and even the craving of your taste buds.

Using the same products and following the same lifestyle pattern has proven to be one of the worst things you could do to your body.

While seasonal changes and your body's reaction to them are inevitable, you can change your lifestyle to be the best version of you throughout the year.

Let's look at it this way—what's the fun in following the same pattern throughout the year anyway?

Our skin and body demand change as per the weather. For example, won't you just kill for some *pakodas* when it's raining outside? Or, given that it's cold in winters, can you resist having your favourite ice cream? And knowing how bad sodas are, don't you just not care in summers?

But let's face it, you are what you eat and I wouldn't give you unreal advice to stop living your life and not have junk food—but ensuring a balance and detoxing your skin and system from time to time is the key to reversing damages done by your culinary indulgences.

Here are some healthy ways to deal with your skin and health throughout the year:

Winter

a. Oily Skin

People with oily skin can take an empty spray container/bottle and fill it with rose water, aloe vera juice and 2 drops of almond oil and spray it to their face—thrice every day. Feel free to carry the bottle along with you in your bag. Following this routine will take off dirt and excess oil, leaving your face adequately moisturized throughout the season.

b. Dry Skin

You know how dry skin can start acting up, especially in winters. But overdosing it with too much cream and oil isn't the solution either. Fix dryness without making your skin get too greasy by pouring some glycerine, rose water, lemon juice and 3 drops of almond oil in a small bottle and let it soak some indirect sunlight for 2–3 days straight.

Use this solution as a night serum and rinse the next morning to keep your skin glowing and hydrated throughout the snowflakes season.

c. Combination Skin

Having combination skin is like being the middle child. You sure have some perks of it, but most of the time, you really can't decide which side you belong to. Settle the dilemma of at-times-too-oily and at-times-too-dry skin by repeating the same recipe as above without almond oil.

d. Concoction for winter

There's never a bad time to drink carrot, beetroot and spinach juice, but in winters, you can boost your glow and keep health in check by drinking this juice by adding pepper and ginger to them. This juice also helps better your vision and soothes a sore throat.

During the chills, one should also eat dry fruits such as almonds, walnuts and figs because they have natural oils in them and those oils are needed to regulate parts of the body that crave extra oil in that season.

Summer

a. Oily Skin

Nothing suffers like oily skin in summers. And of course, there's sunburn and tanning to deal with. As people with oily skin have a higher chance of looking younger for longer (or so a study suggests) they also get their fair share of struggles in their teens.

Here's what you can do to restore radiance, hydration and balance in your skin in summers.

Mix watermelon, cucumber juice and rose water with Fuller's earth clay and sandalwood powder and apply it to your face for 25–30 mins. Rinse and apply aloe vera gel to remove tan and grab summer and scorching heat by the throat.

b. Dry Skin

If you think you can ease it up in summers if you have dry skin, you're wrong.

I wish that was the case. But there's never a good time to let go of discipline.

Mix split red lentil powder (*masoor* dal) with peppermint oil and almond oil. Add grinded papaya and banana paste to it and apply to your face. Leave on for over 25 minutes and rinse. Apply some moisturizer and go to sleep to wake up to a smoother skin.

c. Combination Skin

If you have combination skin, here's what you can do to have a good summer.

Mix watermelon juice, rose water, cucumber juice and Fuller's earth clay with honey to make a paste.

Apply it to your face and leave on for 30 mins. Rinse and moisturize your face.

d. What to Drink

Drink watermelon juice first thing every morning.

Have papaya, cucumber and apple before lunch to ensure you have smoother digestion and a happier gut. These fruits and veggies also have plenty of water in them that'll keep you from getting dehydrated.

Add peppermint leaves to your green tea to feel refreshed all day and get your dose of antioxidants on the go.

Monsoons

This season is mostly kind to your facial skin, but other parts of the body are more prone to infection, inflammation and rashes.

So, here's what you can do to keep your skin happy during the monsoons (for every skin type):

- Put neem leaves, basil leaves and a sliced lemon in a nylon mesh bag and zip it.
- Dip the bag in a bucket full of water and leave it overnight.
- Bathe with the water the next day.

Neem has purifying properties and basil fights pigmentation, lemon cleanses the skin and prevents body odour. And the ingredients combined help keep inflammation, rashes, boils and redness at bay.

Now that you know what to wash your body with in the rainy season, let's skip to haircare.

Even though we feel the minimum need for conditioners in this season, the weather tends to make your hair sticky.

So here's a pre-shampoo hair mask that'll help you fix the stickiness:

- Mix gram flour and curd and create a paste.
- Apply that on your scalp and leave it on for 20 minutes.
- Rinse with a mild shampoo, followed by your favourite conditioner.

And you'd be wrong if you think I would miss face masks for the season just because I said it's not as harsh. Here's what every skin type needs to do in this season:

a. Oily Skin

- To tone your face, start by taking out leaves from a used green tea bag. Mix them with Fuller's earth clay, sandalwood powder, rose water and 4 drops of lemon juice.
- Apply the mask on your face and leave it on for 15 minutes.
- Rinse and apply a light serum.

b. Dry Skin

- Soak red lentils in water and grind.
- Add a few drops of lemon juice, rose water and glycerine/almond oil to it.
- Apply the paste to your face and rinse after 25 minutes.

This paste will make your skin feel balanced in rainy seasons. Following this procedure before bed will make you wake up with a healthy glow and well-hydrated skin.

c. Combination Skin

If you have combination skin, you can just follow the same recipe as for dry skin by adding honey instead of glycerine/almond oil and pink rose petals.

d. What to Drink

- Boil water and add *desi gulab* petals, cinnamon powder, basil leaves, mint leaves and hibiscus petals.
- Filter and pour the concoction in a cup, add lemon juice and dip a tea bag in.

Drink this twice a day to boost metabolism, shield your health from seasonal problems and cleanse your body.

11

Peels

Are you peelin' it?

Is there any satisfaction bigger than giving a second life to resources? Here I'm not talking about recycling plastic cutlery from your take out (although, that's a sensible thing to do) but foods!

The way in fashion an old pair of denims becomes a yoga mat holder if you cut it in half and sew the vertical and horizontal openings, or a skirt becomes a purse if you close the hem and add a sling, there's always an alternate use for most of the things that we throw in our bins.

As per a report[1] published in *The CSR Journal, food worth* Rs 50,000 crore that is produced is wasted every year in our country. Alarming, right?

---

[1] https://thecsrjournal.in/food-wastage-in-india-a-serious-concern/

So, you know you're not the only one who over-purchases vegetables and fruits that are often left in the fridge, and taken out after they are *almost* good for nothing, only to be thrown into the trash can.

So this book is not just about enhancing beauty off your kitchen items, but also cultivating good thoughts, feeling better about yourself, doing your bit to preserve the environment. And these may have been in theory for quite a while, but contributing as little as 10 per cent to the above-mentioned things will change the way you are, and how you feel, react and grow.

Movies, where a young lead character, who does not know what he is doing with his life, somehow ends up with an orphan infant. Initially he has no clue about what needs to be done but, eventually, he rises to the occasion, becoming a power parent in the process and gaining complete control of their lives. It's the high we get from watching something being saved, nurtured and moulded into its best potential.

Another case in point—superhero movies! Everyone loves a hero, but not everyone knows that they're also inside them. So stop looking and start being. Meaning, don't waste food, have your sister's back, process healthy thoughts and watch the beauty of transformation take over.

After all, taking serious things seriously does not make you uncool—that's the thought you need to start with.

This chapter is dedicated to using fruits, vegetables and their peels to help reduce organic wastage and boost your beauty quotient.

1. Tomato Peel

Boil tomatoes and separate the peel from them. Like tomato juice helps get rid of tan, tomato peel too is great to treat blemishes.

2. Potato Peel

A vegetable that's a part of nearly every other cuisine ever made is a natural bleaching agent. And since every house has lots of potato peels coming off every day, you can place these peels under your eyes to reduce puffiness and dark circles.

3. Beetroot Peel

Who doesn't want rosy lips? More so if you can get them without using a tint. That's what beetroot peels are for. Get rosy cheeks and lips by rubbing this peel on your lips and cheeks.

4. Bitter Gourd

You might hate eating this, or worse having *karele ka juice*, but you can massage your skin with its peel to fight dullness.

5. Yam Peel

Yam is rich in Vitamin A. Which means it'll help boost collagen and treat wrinkles, crow's feet and pigmentation.

6. *Radish Peel*

Having radishes makes your skin glow, but even using the peel on your skin helps fight acne and remove blackheads.

7. *Cucumber Peel*

Relaxation doesn't come easier than this. Place cucumber peels on your eyes and lie down for a few minutes. The cooling properties of cucumber helps relieve tired eyes.

8. *Lemon Peel*

This has a number of uses. You use the peel not only on your face, but also on your nails, elbows and feet. You can use it as a scrub by massaging it gently on your face. You can whiten your nails by applying the peel on them and keep your elbows supple by cupping them with a half-cut juiced lemon.

9. *Kiwi Peel*

Apply kiwi peel to your face to cleanse and keep acne at bay. Kiwi is rich in Vitamin C and is great for rejuvenating the skin and keeping excess oil out of the picture.

10. *Orange Peel*

This peel can be used to fight blackheads and acne. You can dry it and use it as a body, hand and foot scrub.

When paired with milk, curd or cream, it can also help get rid of tan.

11. Pomegranate Peel

Using this peel can help prevent wrinkles, acne and some other common skin issues. But drying the peel and grinding to make a powder out of it can be a natural sunscreen if some honey and tomato juice is mixed with that powder.

12. Avocado Peel

It's a freaky goldmine of antioxidants. Not that apple and kiwi aren't, but using avocado peel on your face acts as a natural sunscreen. And since it has good fat, which is good for your face, it helps moisturize your face as well.

13. Apricot Peel

We've all bought apricot scrubs at some point, only because this fruit is capable of solving most of our skin problems. Apricot peel heals irritated skin, helps fight ageing and boosts skin radiance.

14. Banana Peel

Stop throwing away ripe bananas. The peel (along with the ripe fruit) helps smoothen the skin. The peel also helps reduce redness, fine lines and the appearance of acne scars.

15. *Papaya Peel*

Papaya peel helps prevent sagging skin, lightens skin tone and moisturizes it. A special enzyme, papain, found in papaya skin soothes sunburnt skin and helps generate cell renewal.

12

Roots

If this book is named *Roots to Radiance*, it is mandatory not to miss the topic of roots itself. But apart from roots meaning base, it also refers to the strength that it has, the power to hold trees upright and make them stand strong. It is the truest example of how having goodness and power within is one's ultimate strength.

Using the power of roots that keeps the nature upright can fulfil a whole lot of wellness and skincare needs. It grows trees that have leaves, stems, herbs, fruits, flowers and all the possible answers to cure our everyday problems only if we're curious enough to find them.

A lot of vegetables that we use in cooking are actually roots . . . for example, carrot, radish, ginger, turmeric, etc., and a lot of juices we drink are from stems, example sugarcane.

All roots are great for your hair! Why? Because what roots do is make plants grow, and the similar philosophy applies to the roots of your hair. Applying these roots to your scalp in the following ways will treat balding, and it's just one of the many benefits.

In other chapters, I have discussed using most of these ingredients in recipes for good hair and skin. Here I'm going to list the medicinal value and benefits of those roots, stems and leaves and how to use them to sustain good health and peace.

Bonus: They're all already in your house! If they aren't, start buying or growing them right away!

1. Ginger

This root is as good for your skin, as it is for your hair, health and food. Adding a kick to your food since forever, ginger has inflammatory, anti-ageing capabilities, which also contribute to cellulite fading, scar healing and other problems that mean a great deal to you. It definitely makes it to the list of the most inexpensive options to address your health concerns.

- Improve skin tone and elasticity by applying the juice on the areas that suffer from pigmentation and scarring, every day to improve skin health in weeks.
- Mix coconut oil, ginger juice and lemon juice and apply to cellulites to make them fade faster.
- Nourishing the scalp to boost hair growth. Slice a ginger root into pieces and put in a blender. Once blended, extract the juice and mix 2 teaspoons olive oil with it and apply to bald spots on your

scalp to promote new growth. Ginger feeds your follicles and fights free radicals.

2. *Turmeric*

Turmeric is a member of the ginger family. If you look up images of *khadi haldi* on the Internet, you'll see that it even looks like a younger, premature version of ginger. It's a fabulous antiseptic and antibacterial that can sterilize acne, burns and wounds. It is an active ingredient when it comes to fighting zits, cough, arthritis and various kinds of cancer. With its anti-inflammatory capabilities, it can treat redness and rashes in a jiffy.

- Add 2 teaspoons of powdered turmeric to boiling water, mix well and wait for it to cool down. Apply that water to rashes or eczema to treat it fast.
- Mix raw milk, raw honey, ginger and turmeric juice together and apply it to scalp to reverse premature balding.
- Mix extra virgin coconut oil, one teaspoon powdered turmeric and extracts of a Vitamin E capsule to make a crack healing mask for heels.
- Mix turmeric and milk to create a thick paste and apply it to your toenails as an antibacterial.

3. *Sweet Potato*

Shakarkandi is a very popular street food in India. Apart from being delicious and healthy, it is equally good for your skin. Inexpensive, efficient, easy-to-make, there's nothing I don't like about sweet potato. Just like regular potato that grows underground, sweet potato is no different. Dusty pink and the size of half a banana, the endless benefits of this root are no reflection on its size and appearance.

- Slicing and applying its juice on your face minimizes pigmentation.
- We talk a lot about polycystic ovaries but not enough about fibrocystic breasts. These are lumps in your breasts that can lead to cancer. Boiling sweet potatoes in water and then adding lemon and rock salt to it before consumption is an anti-ageing ritual that also reduces the formation of lumps and keeps you younger. Don't throw away the water though.
- Soak your feet in the water that boiled sweet potatoes to treat cracked heels. It'll be better if you can also add sea salt to it, though that is optional.

4. Carrot

Low blood pressure, dehydration, ageing, poor vision—you name it, this root has a solution to a number of problems. Carrot is also an anti-cancer root that makes for adequate fibre content when consumed in proper proportions. It is also packed with beta carotene and potassium, which people with oily skin can benefit from. Drinking a glass of carrot juice every morning can reduce chances of cancer remarkably and also prevent sun damage super effectively.

- Apply carrot juice on your face for 20 minutes to eliminate excess oil. Wash off and repeat thrice a week.
- Blend a couple of carrots, make a paste and apply to face to reduce blemishes. Rinse after 20 minutes. Repeat twice/thrice a week.
- Add curd and 1 tablespoon cucumber extract to boiled and mashed carrots, mix and apply to your hair to make them more manageable and to beat frizziness and unruly hair.

5. Beetroot

Not just skincare, this root can even replace some of your chemical-packed cosmetics like lip/cheek tint and hair colour . . . and so some of the recipes in the previous chapters of this book have taught you. Apart from being superficial substitutes, beetroots (*chukandar*) can help treat arthritis, kidney stones, low blood pressure, menopausal struggles, burns, anaemia and so on . . .

Eating or drinking beetroot juice everyday can also stabilize your period cycle and ensure proper digestion.

- Mix henna powder, curd, and beetroot juice and make a paste. Apply to hair for one hour and wash off to chase away dandruff. Do this once a week.

- Drink a glass or two every day to keep ovarian cysts at bay.
- Apply beetroot juice to your lips daily to make them pinker.

6. *Radish*

This root is majorly detoxifying. And apart from clearing complexion and treating hairfall, this root can treat one of the most common problems in our generation—insomnia!

Radish makes bones healthy and drinking its juice can help keep kidneys clean and treat urine infections.

- Prevent blackheads by applying radish juice on your face twice a week.
- Mix 2 tablespoons radish juice with onion soup or beetroot juice and drink daily to calm your nervous system and sleep better.
- Apply radish juice to scalp to remove dandruff and boost hair growth.

7. *Onion*

Time and again, we are reminded of the importance of this root in our lives. Just eating it raw can kill most germs in our mouth and stomach. But there's more to onion than its germ-fighting capabilities.

An antioxidant, anti-allergic, that has cholesterol-controlling abilities, and several things that I'm about to tell you will make you crying while chopping it not sound so bad.

- Apply onion juice on your face to reduce acne and blemishes.
- Apply onion juice to your scalp for half an hour before you rinse with shampoo to reverse balding drastically faster.
- Reverse damage done to your eyes by screen exposure of mobiles and computers by mixing two drops of onion juice, two drops of lemon juice, two drops of ginger juice with one teaspoon honey . . . mix well with one cup of water. Now you have a DIY eyedrop ready to reduce eye irritation and redness.

8. Garlic

Yes, it's that ingredient which when added to toasted bread and cheese takes you to heaven. The way it zests food proves the power of how these ingredients can enhance a formula. Now whether it's about enhancing a food recipe or using these ingredients to improve wellness and beauty concerns, these easily available roots clearly have the power to transform you. Topping it all off is the libido-boosting, fungal infection fighting and life-simplifying qualities of garlic.

- Place a garlic clove under your teeth to prevent toothache.

- Crush garlic and apply its juice to prevent acne, irritation and blemishes.
- Mash three garlic pods, mix them with water and drink the concoction. Garlic's antibacterial, antifungal properties chase away infections of any kind.

9. Turnip

Turnip is a rich source of dietary fibres, Vitamin C and collagen-generating elements. It also helps to lose weight. It makes you feel full without consuming too many extra calories. It is rich in iron and, when juiced, it can provide UV protection against sun damage.

Eating turnips, cucumbers, carrots, beetroots and sweet potatoes together as a salad can cure a number of health issues. This is something you should add to your diet immediately.

- Rub a sliced turnip in your underarms after bathing to block body odour.
- Add more turnips to your diet to boost your metabolism and feel fuller without having to eat too much, and hence end up consuming fewer calories.
- Boil turnips and use them in your diet somehow. There are plenty of recipes available for turnips. However, don't throw away the water—apply it to your face and body to have a collagen-packed wash and boost cell renewal.

10. Celery

Celery root is the cutest addition to this list. This root looks like a white bulb that is totally Instagrammable. Posting healthy #InstaFood every once in a while is good for the health of your feed after all. Powdered celery is a big hit in the wellness market right now. People are having it first thing in the morning with their first glass of water to speed up metabolism and lose weight. But the benefits of celery roots aren't limited to the weight loss territory. It's much more crucial than that. Since this is a beauty book, here's what you can do with celery:

- Boil celery in 1 cup water and drink the tea. Doing so cures peptic ulcers and stomach sores.
- Grind and drink its juice every day to kickstart your day with a blast of energy.
- Apply celery juice to your face to help restore youth without having to do too much.

13

Clays and Muds

Roots grow beneath the soil, and while in the previous chapter I suggested that you derive radiance from the roots, it's a given that I would like to talk about the importance of the land it grows under as well.

My mother always says that if you have to judge the properties of a vegetable or a herb, look at the shape, nature and appearance of it to guess its benefits.

A bottle gourd (*Lauki*) is one of the longest vegetables, so if it's in its nature to grow long, it can help you increase your height if it's fed to you as a kid. Beet is red in colour—so when it's infused with water, tea or wax, it can be a cheek/lip tint or a hair colour, etc.

Studying the nature of nature's components is a beautiful activity. It's a hobby as beautiful as birdwatching, wildlife photography, researching historical findings, and many other examples of fulfilling pleasures we like to invest in, in downtime.

Now, I won't make this seem like you're in a science class, but there's no denying that understanding the benefits of natural ingredients *is* science. Reading this book is understanding science, practising the methods in it is science, formulating your own recipes is science . . .

You are a result of nature and science after all. Even though you hate having to memorize the periodic table in chemistry and laws of physics, you're totally going to love the knowledge I'm about to share on using different kinds of clays and muds to your advantage.

If these clays can grow medicinal plants in them, protect them from the dangers of the environment and mature them to the point that they qualify to be used for medicines that save lives and recipes to benefit humankind, they can fix your concerns.

If soil can nurture and guard its plants like a mother, it can definitely take care of your skin, hair and health.

Clays and muds are dominant ingredients in most of the face and hair masks available in the market today. Volcanic clay, Fuller's earth, Kaolin clay, Bentonite clay, Volcanic mud—the list goes on . . . Fresh and damp or powdered for storage, clays hardly have an expiry date and never lose their efficiency. Even if you move it to another location, it'll start doing what it does best from the new spot, i.e., producing!

Across the book I have explained the importance of clays that you can use to treat skin and body concerns at home, but this chapter is mostly for you to understand how to incorporate and formulate your own recipes by understanding what's best for your skin.

So, feel free to collect these muds and clays whenever you spot them next. Every region and country has their own special kinds of rocks, clays and plants that are good for you in some way or the other. If you're a real beauty enthusiast like me, you'll do your due diligence in advance when taking a vacation and making the most out of it.

The mere use of mud and clays is to sculpt them and make sculptures, so if you aren't sculpting your face while you globetrot, are you even living the good life?

Here are some commonly available and some never-heard-before masks that you should add to your bag the moment you spot them:

1. French Green Clay (Pore-tightening face mask)

Also known as Sea Clay, Marine Clay and Illite Clay

Heading to Europe? Do try out French green clay that is found in huge parts of Europe. Or just try seeing if you can get genuine quality clay online. The reason it's called French Green Clay is because the green colour comes from decomposed plant matter and iron oxide. This clay can absorb oils like you can finish a pizza!

French Green Clay is best suited for people who struggle with open pores and oily skin.

Mixing it with rose water can chase away all your oily skin struggles with its absorbent powers—if it's truly green in colour, that is. Do not buy it if it isn't green. The green pigment itself is a proof of plant matter absorption, so if it is grey, look for better quality.

2. Rhassoul Clay (Detoxifying scrub, hair mask)

Also known as Moroccan Lava Clay, Moroccan Red Clay and Ghassoul Clay

Have a friend who's coming back from Morocco? Ask them to help you eliminate blackheads by getting this humble clay for you. Or just buy it online from a reliable source.

This clay goes by the name Ghassoul in Morocco, but is identified as 'Rhassoul' globally.

Blackheads on follicles and open pores lead to excess sebum secretion, making your face look greasy and grey just a few hours after you do your make-up. While the night is still young, you want to run away like Cinderella because you feel like your face is giving up.

- Mix rhassoul clay with apple cider vinegar and red lentil powder and massage your face with that paste to clear your face weekly.
- If you have an oily scalp, make a very thin paste of rhassoul clay and water and massage your scalp with it before shampooing.

3. Hungarian Moor Mud

Also known as European Moor Mud, Balneo-Peat and Peat Moss

Okay, so this peat moss can get you a glowing body like Kate Moss in no time, puns aside . . . this is a mud many celebrities have recommended getting spa treatments with.

It contains almost no clay and is found mostly in the Czech Republic and Hungary. Its skin-replenishing abilities are a result of natural decomposition of plants and grasses. This healing mud is rich in vitamins, minerals, amino acids and organic enzymes.

Its benefits are so vast that luxury spas recommend going for an immersion bath treatment with it.

This healing mask when applied to body can detoxify, improve blood circulation and help achieve smoother skin. And the best part is, it completely dissolves in water.

4. Umbrian Clay

Umbrian clay is an umbrella for your skin . . . meaning, it can shield you from having any more acne, blemishes and rosacea. Many skincare companies are making crazy bucks out of selling this clay for its purifying, mineral-rich properties. It is pistachio-green in colour and is found in Umbria, Italy.

Just mixing water with this clay and applying it to your face regularly will erase blemishes fast.

5. French Pink Clay

Also known as Rose Clay

Much like the French green clay, this is also found in Europe and is pink in colour. This clay has the power to smoothen and polish your skin without a fuss. This mask is rich in iron and can make the roots of your hair stronger and help delay greying.

- Just mixing green tea with this clay and adding a few drops of rosehip oil in it can brighten your face and fight wrinkles with minimal efforts.
- Applying the same mask to your hair (without the rosehip oil) can prevent scalp irritation and make your hair darker and stronger.

6. Alpine Forest Mud

Also known as Alpine Moor Mud

As the name suggests, this mud is found in the Alpine forests. The miraculous combination of carbon compounds in this mud has a gentle effect on your body while cleaning it really thoroughly. So if you're looking to switch your soaps with something that'll cleanse your body without being too harsh, *this is it!* Just apply it directly to do a deep cleanse.

7. Cambrian Blue Clay

This clay is said to be the oldest blue clay known to mankind. A master in restoring youth and renewing skin cells, this clay is big in the medicine industry as well. Known for treating rosacea, arthritis and diabetes, this star clay is found by the salt lakes of Siberia.

It can remove toxins and bacteria in a wash and repair the damages of make-up and harmful chemicals transferred into your skin by pollution and heat.

- Dip a chamomile tea bag in boiled water for a few minutes, then add the tea to this clay to make a paste out of it, and apply to face to slow down ageing.
- You can also make soaps out of this one by adding castile soap and beeswax (as explained in the lip balm, body washes section).

8. Icelandic Silica Mud

This clay, as the name suggests, is found in Iceland. It is actually found in one of the most popular destinations in that country—the Blue Lagoon—and is rich in silica.

This mud is mostly used for its anti-ageing paste that boosts the skin to produce more collagen and new skin cells.

Just applying a thin layer of this mud can help you fight ageing like a charm. All muds and clays are soothing and their functions are also quite similar.

9. Yellow Kaolin Clay

The benefits of white kaolin clay, aka *cheeni mitti*, have been explained in other chapters. Fuller's earth, kaolin clay and black soil are a few ingredients we have talked about in the recipes of previous chapters, but what hasn't been covered is these few types of kaolin clay that you can also buy if you think you have the following skin concerns—dry and sensitive skin, poor blood circulation levels and uneven face texture.

This clay looks a lot like turmeric, and was found in China years ago. It is easily available in India now and can be bought online too.

- Crush neem leaves in a mortar and pestle and then boil them in a cup of water. Filter out the leaves and use this water to make a paste of yellow kaolin clay and apply to face. Wash once it has dried and follow it up with a face serum.

10. Red Kaolin Clay

Another product from China but available globally, red kaolin clay is ideal for people who have puffiness-prone skin. It also treats rashes and burns.

- Take around 20 basil leaves and crush them with a mortar and pestle. When you're done, add those crushed leaves to boiled water and wait for a few minutes for the mixture to cool down.
- Then use that water and red kaolin clay to make a paste and apply to face. Wash when it dries and apply serum. You can also apply this (like all the other masks) to your body if you're struggling with the same problem as your face anywhere on your body.

11. Dead Sea Mud

If floating on the dead sea without sinking is on your bucket list, make sure you fill that bucket with the sea's mud on your way back. Why, you ask? That mud is a true multitasker.

It can even your skin tone, treat acne, remove harmful toxins, dirt and impurities, improve texture and reduce redness. All this while maintaining the pH balance and more.

This is an evergreen all-purpose mask for face and body. The greenish grey mud also makes the skin more elastic and doesn't need a second ingredient if it's fresh.

If you're buying a powdered version online, mix it with water to make a face and body mask you can apply for 20 minutes before bathing. Rinse and follow up with your favourite creams.

14

Infused Waters

Moms can get persuasive about your hydration needs. And I did a terrible job at keeping my system hydrated until a few years ago. A funny thing happened a few months ago when my mum visited me in Delhi. Even though I thought I had become better at drinking enough water throughout the day, somehow it had to go wrong when someone was watching! Obviously!

So I was at home on a Sunday finishing some work and on her watch I did not have water for about six hours straight, and she reminded me to drink water, also accusing me of lying about getting better at this. My skin had become all red because of dehydration and my mother couldn't believe how I could do this to myself.

Obviously, I didn't have a very strong case to argue so I just went about following my general Monday schedule the next day, and I received a text from her every two hours saying, 'Drink water'.

Honestly, I would like to start a support group for busy, dehydrated women. I mean, it isn't easy to keep up with your day-to-day work, social life, running errands, pursuing ambitions, excelling at tasks at hand and trying our best to drink water.

It is tasteless, odourless, colourless and still runs our life!

We need to pep up this activity for us to be able to stay hydrated. Because let's admit it, we take water for granted. If we don't end up drinking all of it from our bottles, we feed it to the plants, or just throw it and refill our bottle again, never having the intention to finish all of it.

But if only we made this activity more fun, our approach could change. Putting a tad more effort to make water infused with our favourite ingredients can add antioxidants, Vitamin C and other benefitting ingredients to water. And let's be honest, when we're putting this much effort to fill a glass jug or a mason jar with water, we'd hate to watch it go to waste, hence will end up finishing it. My dermat Dr Geetika Mittal Gupta is such an infused waters enthusiast. I love how every corner of her clinic has a new combination of these waters.

It's a trick to making yourself drink more water with added ingredients that are good for your system and skin. Here are some easy-to-make infused water recipes that'll force you to become a hydrate enthusiast!

Just one little request: if you want to sweeten it, don't add sugar . . . try honey, jaggery or other forms of 'natural', non-fattening ingredients. Take this as making drinking water more exciting than anything else.

1. Cucumber + Lemon + Mint

This is a great one, especially for the summers when our body gets severely dehydrated by the scorching heat. These are all cooling ingredients that'll relax your body and keep you energized.

Slice or grate one full cucumber and add the juice of half a lemon and 25 mashed mint leaves in a glass jar filled with water. Drink all day to relax your system, keep metabolic rates up and maintain good skin.

2. Blueberry + Orange + Cinnamon

This one will charge your metabolism with a blast of Vitamin C and antioxidants.

Add a cup of crushed blueberries, 4 slices of peeled oranges and 1 teaspoon cinnamon powder in a glass jar full of water. Drink throughout the day.

3. Strawberry + Kiwi + Lime

Slice 3 strawberries, 2–3 kiwis and half a lime and add them all to a glass jar filled with water. Drink all day. This too will hydrate your skin and system with its Vitamin C and antioxidant content.

4. Cherry + Basil

Basil has high anti-inflammatory properties that'll soothe your stomach, more so if you love spicy food.

Cherry will help you get a good night's rest and lower blood sugar levels.

Add a cup of sliced cherries and 20 roughly mashed basil leaves in a jar and drink all day.

5. Pineapple + Coconut

The whole idea behind this is to give you the pleasure of a Piña Colada without the alcohol and useless calories. Take off the shell of the coconut and slice off 3–4 pieces of it and of pineapple, and add it all to a glass jar full of water. Drink throughout the day without guilt. This water is also good for those trying to keep their weight in check without making the skin suffer.

6. Raspberry + Grapefruit + Rosemary

Applying rosemary to skin and hair has been discussed often in this book. Now it's time to drink it too, for its cancer and heart diseases fighting ingredients—not to forget skin hydrants.

Slice 5 raspberries and a grapefruit and dip them in a glass jar full of water along with 5 sprigs of rosemary. Drink all day.

7. Apple + Green Apple + Ginger

If an apple a day keeps the doctor away, imagine what two apples can do.

Slice one red and one green apple and add them to a jar full of water along with half a teaspoon of grated ginger. Sip all day. This water has ageing-fighting, nausea-relieving ingredients.

8. Pomegranate + Hibiscus + Beetroot

Better digestion, anti-ageing, bone-strengthening, full of antioxidants—this recipe is for winners!

Add pomegranate seeds, the petals of one hibiscus, and one grated beetroot to a jar full of water. Sip throughout the day.

9. Aloe + Jujube

Aloe vera soothes the stomach and improves digestion and skin from within. Jujube helps relieve anxiety and regulates blood pressure. Add half a cup of aloe vera extract to a cup of sliced jujubes in a jar filled with water and drink all day.

Remember: There are two types of aloe vera—one that can be eaten and one that can be applied on the skin. Pick the right one for the respective recipe.

10. Blackberry + Lemongrass

Boost brain health with added benefits of manganese and Vitamin K, among other things, from blackberries, and help menstrual pain, speed up metabolism and burn fat with lemongrass in this detox recipe. Add 1 cup sliced blackberries and 4 sprigs of lemongrass in water and sip all day.

You can totally switch the ingredients according to your liking to come up with your own recipes.

Detox away!

15

Under Three-Minute Hacks

None of us can turn down a tip that benefits our health and takes minimum time to do so. And to fight our skin and health issues with just a couple of ingredients is such a win-win. But here's what you need to know— not every DIY tip has to have an elaborate list of ingredients, although that doesn't make it any less filled with goodness.

As Yvon Chouinard rightly said, 'Going back to a simpler life is not a step backward.' How can it be?

The year 2019 glorified this new term called 'JOMO' (Joy of Missing Out), an antonym of 'FOMO' (Fear of Missing Out). Didn't your best friend say that she had serious FOMO when you chilled with your other besties without her? Well, this year has taught us to embrace the opposite.

With all those memes about celebrating cancelled plans, doing absolutely nothing on weekends and keepin' it #LowKey, the fellowship is hinting on resorting to simpler choices to unlock the secrets to feeling truly liberated. But while we're *Netflix*ing our way through the weekend, sparing a minute or two to treat skin and health concerns does not seem like a bad idea at all.

While writing this chapter, what I kept in mind are things we can do without actually taking out time for them. Often, I would see my mum apply organic ingredients on her face while working in the kitchen. A ripe banana that no one was having was actually one of the best masks to restore the glow and smoothness on the face. This way she never had to take out time for masking . . . she just mashed and applied it while working and rinsed it when she was done in the kitchen.

A used green tea bag in an empty cup could be used both to fertilize plants and to treat puffy eyes. While I'm giving out tips to be your best beautiful with the help of natural ingredients and help keep it cost-efficient, I thought, why not have a list of hacks that will also keep it time-efficient?

One of the many plus sides to productivity is that it goes hand in hand with happiness and contentment. For instance, won't you have the best Monday ever if you arranged your closet, cleaned your house, got your dose of long due beauty sleep, masked your face and got a hair spa the day before? I know, Monday would still be Monday, but feeling gorgeous and being sorted will make you feel so much lighter.

And in this day and age, organic hacks that are pocket-friendly and don't even take a lot of time are an idea we millennials can totally chase.

And while we are at it, let's discuss some three-minute healthy alternatives you should add to your routine to max out the power of holistic beauty.

1. Smoothen you face in minutes before applying make-up

Our skin tends to get tired of being painted with make-up every day. So kiss and make-up with your skin by showing it some love before applying foundation.

Mix 1 teaspoon honey with 1 tablespoon raw milk and apply it to your face. Keep it on for a minute or two and then rinse with lukewarm water.

The effects of milk and honey will make your skin feel even and moisturized. After that, your foundation will do a better job at blending on your face.

2. Get amazing lashes without using a mascara . . .

. . . but with a mascara wand. Never throw out mascara wands after the product is over. There are so many ways to use them. For instance, this one: mix castor oil, avocado oil and coconut oil in a small bottle and apply that to your lashes with a clean mascara wand. This will give your lashes an instant lift and will also make them grow faster. You can also use this oil to set the baby hair on your crown area and help stop balding. You can grow bushy brows if you're into that by applying the same oil on the wand and brush your brow hair with it. This will not only help shape the growth of your brows but will help form a smooth base for your eyebrow pencil to glide on.

3. Remove upper lip/eyebrow hair with this homemade wax

It's infuriating when you need to head out for an important meeting or a date, and your favourite salon can't give you an appointment. So here's what you can do to deal with that situation at home:

Simmer ½ cup water with ½ cup sugar, lemon juice and coconut oil. When it's fully heated, pour it in a container—and your wax is ready. Use a spatula to apply on to the areas you want to wax.

4. Use the healthiest lip and cheek tint

Looking great all the time gives you a certain kind of high. And with the help of all-natural products, you can have a blush on your cheeks and tint on your lips without harming your skin or using chemicals. Here's how: grate a peeled beetroot for a few seconds—even that much should be enough to produce the juice you need to give the hint of pink to your lips and cheeks.

5. Exfoliate your lips in a jiffy

Stop complaining about your lipsticks not lasting long enough. The reason could be that you're not exfoliating your lips. In order to make your lipstick stay longer, you need to remove the dead skin time to time. Add sugar to coconut oil and massage your lips gently. After 1–3 minutes, take a warm, damp cloth or dry tissue to wipe off the extra oil. Coconut oil is a great alternative to make-up removers as well.

6. Deodorize your armpits without using a flammable deodorant

Tired of that burning sensation you get after spraying a deodorant on your freshly shaved armpits? Well, chuck that! Here's how you can deodorize your armpits with natural ingredients.

Take a few spoons of bentonite clay and mix lemon juice and rose water with it. Apply that paste to your armpits and wipe it with a warm, wet towel.

7. A lazy girl's toner

I call it a lazy girl's toner because it literally requires you to mix water and apple cider vinegar in a 1:1 ratio to come up with the easiest solution that'll tone your skin in no time. Using this in the morning and at night before sleeping will energize your skin.

8. Ditch hair serum for this oil

Mix 2 drops of jojoba oil in your palms and apply it to the dry ends of your hair to moisturize them. Unlike serums, hair oils help repair your hair in ways a serum won't. Use just the minimum amount to nourish the ends; if you overdo it, it can make your hair look oily. If you're doing this before you shampoo, you can go ahead and oil your hair properly to make your hair more manageable and silkier post wash.

9. Scrub and exfoliate your body with this two-ingredient scrub

Keep collecting coffee grounds from the remains of your everyday coffee. Mix the coffee grounds with coconut oil and gently massage your body to exfoliate dead skin and get smoother body texture. The coarseness of coffee grounds helps exfoliate and polish your body.

10. Not just coffee, save your green tea bags as well!

Don't toss the bags out of your morning and evening green tea cups. Refrigerate the tea bag after you're done sipping your morning tea. When you're about to end the day, take out that used green tea bag from the refrigerator and rest it on your eyes for 2 mins each. The natural tannin present in green tea helps treat puffy eyes and dark circles.

11. Make your hands soft instantly

This may be one of the easiest hacks. Just pluck a marigold (*genda*), remove the petals and mash them with your hands. Apply the nectar all over your hands—that's all. The nectar of this flowers makes for a great hand salve for skin. You can also use this to cure rashes and minor wounds.

12. Fix scalp greasiness with this DIY dry shampoo

Apply cocoa powder (if your hair is black or brunette) or cornstarch (if it's blond) directly to your scalp and brush it off with a hair brush. This will not only clear out excess oil and absorb the greasiness but also help add volume to your hair.

13. Give natural volume to your lashes by applying petroleum jelly

Wearing mascara can be heavy on your lashes after a while, so on days when you want to say no to make-up but still want to have voluminous lashes, take a cotton earbud and apply a thin layer of petroleum jelly on your lashes. This will give it an instant volume naturally, and help it grow too! Win-win!

14. Flatten a pimple overnight

Garlic has anti-fungal and drying qualities. Slicing the head off a garlic clove and applying garlic juice on a pimple can help flatten it overnight.

15. Whiten teeth with baking soda and lemon juice

Add a few drops of lemon juice to 1 teaspoon baking soda in a non-metal plate to make a paste. Clean excess saliva from your mouth and teeth with a tissue and dip your toothbrush in the paste and brush your teeth with it for 2 minutes. Rinse your mouth after you're done.

16. Use this one-ingredient scrub mask to exfoliate your skin

Sapodilla, also known as *chikoo*, is such a humble fruit! It tastes yummy, but your face will love it too. Peel the chikoo and take the seeds out, crush the fruit and apply to your face to scrub and mask at the same time. This is quite a multitasker.

17. DIY cleansing milk that puts every expensive make-up remover to shame

Most make-up removers will require you to wash your face after using them. This DIY cleansing milk won't. Mix raw milk, lemon juice, rose water and a few drops of almond oil together and take a cotton pad to remove your make-up with it. This is the only hydrant you need after wearing cosmetics on your face all day.

18. Freshen up your skin on the go

If your face gets dehydrated quickly after you leave your house, pour some distilled water in a spray bottle and add rose petals (desi gulab) to it and carry it in your bag. Spray on your face every once in a while to hydrate your skin on the fly and on the go instantly.

19. Speed up your hair-conditioning routine

Usually a regular conditioner requires you to apply it and wait for a while before you wash it off. But this DIY one only requires you to mix it with water and give it a quick wash. Add 1 cup apple cider vinegar to 1 cup water in a mug and run it through your hair thoroughly before rinsing.

20. Make an organic hairspray that won't harm your hair

Usually after you use heat, using a hairspray is just another addition to the damage you're already putting your hair through. This damage is usually done by straightening, curling and blow dry. So instead, make braids and leave them overnight, and when you open them in the morning, set them with this DIY hair spray: Mix 2 teaspoons of sea salt with 50 ml carbonated water, and pour it in a spray bottle. This should be able to hold your curls without harming them.

21. Reduce redness and inflammation on the skin with one simple trick

Acne can be persuasive sometimes . . . almost all the time. Just reduce the inflammation and swelling with rubbing ice on it for 5–7 minutes at night to flatten it as much as you can overnight.

22. Get a radiant and refreshed body by making an absolutely simple scrub

Party plans that require wearing that backless dress you bought and never wore? Pull it out and take it to town. Mix 2 teaspoons sugar with ½ cup olive oil and 10 drops of peppermint/lavender/spearmint oil. Mix and massage your body before bathing to feel and smell fresh.

23. Heal cracked hands by using this hand salve

Winters can be brutal. No matter how much hand cream you feed to your hands, they always feel dry and ashy. Apply a layer of mayonnaise to your hands and layer it with two teaspoons castor oil. Wash it after a minute to hydrate your skin for a whole day.

24. Moisturize, depigment and even skin tone with one fruit extract

Avocado is the most millennial fruit. It's expensive for all the right reasons, but the surprising thing about it is that it's better to apply as a face mask than to be eaten. Just apply mashed avocado on your face and hydrate, reduce pigmentation, reduce puffiness around eyes and get even skin tone by doing this twice or thrice a week.

25. Treat dry scalp with this easy-to-make oil-in-spray

A few tips ago I suggested a DIY dry shampoo for oily scalp, so naturally dry scalp shouldn't be left out. Mix 10 drops of tea tree oil with 50 ml jojoba oil and pour it in a small spray bottle. Spray this oil to your scalp—it'll barely take two minutes. Follow up with a shampoo whenever you plan to.

26. Make eyelashes longer naturally with this mixture of oils

Remember how I have kept reminding you to save your mascara wands? You'll need a wand for this too. Mix 1 teaspoon castor/coconut oil with 8 drops of lavender oil and blend it. Use the mascara wand to apply that to your lashes thrice a week to grow naturally long lashes.

27. Cleanse pores and dirt off your face with salt water

Sea salt is good for your face. I have talked about using it in your bath and removing facial hair with it as one of the ingredients. You can also deep cleanse your pores and eliminate extra oil and dirt off your face with it. Just pour some lukewarm water in a bowl, add 1 teaspoon sea salt in it and let it dissolve. Take a cotton ball or a clean, soft cloth and dip it in that water and then apply all over your face and neck. If you are using a piece of clean cloth, you can also spread it on your face like a sheet mask for 4 minutes and take it off. After 5 minutes, rinse with regular water.

28. A juicy sun protection

Sunburns happen all the time. Just slice up a tomato and apply its juice all over your face and neck to protect your skin from sunburn.

29. Remove under-eye dark circles and face pigmentation with one ingredient

Puffy, pigmented under-eyes are a proof of our busy and stressful lifestyle. When you get home after a long day, just grate a potato and extract its juice in a small bowl. Take a cotton pad and apply it to your under-eyes and other pigmented areas of your face to even your skin tone over time.

30. Smoothen your face with this ingredient that takes under 10 seconds to prepare—for all skin types

Dull skin? No problem! Either mash up a ripe banana and apply to your face or just apply raw honey to your face. Both these ingredients can smoothen your face without much effort. No matter how your skin is—oily, dry, sensitive—it's good for all!

A recipe that involves using these two ingredients together is also explained in this book.

31. A humble one-ingredient dark spot corrector

Every beauty brand is selling 'sleeping masks' right now. The goal of these masks is to improve skin texture and fight dark spots. What if I told you there's one ingredient that suits all skin types and can fade dark spots over time? Yes, ditch those creams, cut open an aloe vera stem, apply the extract on your face and leave overnight. Rinse next morning like usual.

32. Eliminate blackheads with this three-ingredient paste

Those annoying little blackheads that keep popping up can go away by mixing water, toothpaste and baking soda and applying it on your nose and surrounding areas. Use an old mascara wand or a baby toothbrush to massage the paste on the affected area.

33. Make this one-ingredient hair growth enhancer at home within seconds

We all know onion juice is great for stimulating hair growth and preventing premature balding.

Just slice and grind an onion, and apply its juice on your scalp. Doing this can boost hair growth over time.

34. Beat dry hands in winter

Your hands need way more hydration that you can imagine. In winters when your skin is dry, it needs exfoliation and moisturization. So mix a few tablespoons of olive oil with salt and apply it to your hands. Scrub gently and rinse with only water. This will remove dead skin, leaving your hands feel gentle.

35. Genius scalp exfoliation method that you barely have to put any effort into

Along with your routine shampoo sessions, just add 2 tablespoons white sugar to the shampoo solution. Apply to scalp and massage the sugar to eliminate impurities properly, leaving your scalp healthier. This will also stop your roots from getting oily too soon.

36. Make skin tone even by mixing these two ingredients

Short skirts, sports, sun exposure—there are a lot of factors that lead to making the skin of your elbows and knees uneven. Just mix Fuller's earth clay with apple cider vinegar. Rinse those areas with this mixture and your skin will become supple over time.

37. Treat period cramps by applying this essential oil

Okay, not really beauty-related but so important for most of us! In terms of beauty, pain will cause you to squint, it'll then give you fine lines over time, so you better fix it. Gently rub a few drops of lavender oil on your abdomen to soothe the cramps.

38. Prevent wrinkles and acne by sleeping right

Sleeping on your back is a great thing for your skin if you can manage that. Your face is well rested when it's laying straight all night. This will also keep your face from coming in contact with your pillow case. Not saying your pillow case is dirty, but who wants to take chances—we do take pizza to bed at times.

39. Banish dark circles by mixing these two ingredients

Vitamin E capsules are so cheap. Cut open one capsule and mix it with aloe vera gel and apply around the eyes to fade dark circles.

Talking about under-eye care, a funny thing I learnt about over-eye care from a seventy-eight-year-old glamma, Vera DiLeo on Instagram. She had sound advice for the likes of us. 'Never squint, it causes wrinkles, if you can't see it, you can't see it,' she says.

So on another note, stop squinting no matter what. Fake a smile through those infuriating work mails.

40. Get that beauty sleep you always wanted

Sleeping for eight hours is almost impossible. All the stress and anxiety take over right when you're trying to sleep. Apply some peppermint oil on the temples of your forehead. This will calm your nerves and help you get shut-eye faster.

41. Nourish dry tips of your hair instantly

Hair thinning leads to split ends. It all starts with dry tips of your hair losing weight and volume.

You can bring it back by applying petroleum jelly on the dry ends and combing normally. Just don't use the same comb to brush the scalp, else the scalp gets greasy.

42. Beat redness, wrinkles, acne rosacea and more by applying this oil

Woah! That's a lot of problems solved by one oil. Applying sea buckthorn oil regularly to your face can reduce redness and acne drastically. All you have to do is use this oil after washing your face to moisturize your skin. Leave it on for skin to heal.

43. Drink the purest water

Yes, I'm going *there*. After the world has imposed on you to drink 8–13 glasses of water a day, here's more. Soak basil leaves in your water pitcher to remove about 95 per cent fluoride in it. The result? Better oral health and no cavities.

44. Balance your body's pH levels regularly

This is not as complicated as it sounds. I'm just asking you to drink coconut water every morning. Mornings are the ideal time to drink it, and balancing pH levels does wonders for your skin.

45. Tighten your pores with very little effort

Mix 2 tablespoons tomato juice with few drops of lemon juice and apply to face. This will not only cure sunburn, but will also tighten your pores that secrete sebum and make your skin oily.

46. Another DIY toothpaste for a healthier mouth

Oral health is not to be neglected. Especially if it takes under 3 minutes to take care of it.

Mix coconut oil and turmeric powder to create a paste. Apply it to teeth with a brush and rinse. Turmeric is the antiseptic that'll treat sore gums and clear plague. Coconut oil kills bacteria present in the mouth.

47. Beat mouth and body odour with two ingredients

Add lemon juice to hot water and drink it. This will treat bad breath in a jiffy. Slice a lime and apply to sweat-prone areas before heading out to keep body odour at bay.

48. A four-ingredient detox drink for clearer skin

Add cucumber slices, lemon juice and mint leaves to water and drink it every morning to detox and get clearer skin.

49. Moisturize with avocado juice

Avocado adds fat to your cells. It can help you generate new skin cells, minimize dark circles and soothe your skin. Slice open an avocado and rub it on your face to moisturize the skin deeply and achieve unmatched radiance.

50. Drink enough water

It takes less than 3 minutes to finish a glass—you knew about this one, didn't you? Now, this is something everyone tells you, so let me be more precise, attempt to drink 13–14 glasses of water a day for a week and see how that works out. I frankly couldn't believe my skin when I did that.

Expert Inputs

Sanjeev Kapoor's Recipes

When I started writing this book, I had a vision in place. The aim to have the poster people of each profession to weigh in with their expert advice to help achieve true beauty. One that matches inside with the outside.

While every chapter is a mixture of what you should do, what you should apply, what you should imply, I believe the part about what you should be eating shouldn't be left untouched. What you put in your body is what's going to show on your skin. Don't worry, I won't push you to practise a lifestyle where you can't even live a little. Let's be realistic, let yourself go in limits, have one full cheat day if you like . . .

In this book of millennial content, knowing that we are the most stressed generation, let me give you the freedom to indulge, but also balance it with healthy food, super foods and all good things that'll nourish your body and make it ready for challenges to come.

And there is no one better than top Indian Master Chef Sanjeev Kapoor to school you about this.

This chef extraordinaire, apart from cooking the yummiest food, has written more than 150 cookbooks himself. I remember watching his TV show as a kid for years and being mesmerized by everything he cooked. In this chapter, let the most celebrated chef of this country tell you all about healthy eating.

Super Foods

Today, we have promptly adopted the eating healthy culture and lapped up on trends that focus on health and nutrition, super foods being one of them.

While the term super foods makes it sound like such a Western concept, you'd be surprised to know how many ingredients on global super foods lists are of Indian origin or have been widely used in Indian medicine and food for ages through the ancient Indian doctrine of Ayurveda.

Ayurveda, the world's oldest healing science, is a compilation of the words *ayus*, which means life, and *Veda*, which means knowledge or science. It follows the principle of 'we are what we eat', and uses food to balance the body constitutions or *tridoshas* (*vata*, *pitta*, *kapha*) in an individual, a concept which, as a foodie, chef and practitioner of Ayurveda, I firmly agree with—food is indeed medicine.

Keeping with this theme, I am going to share with you some simple, everyday Ayurvedic ingredients that have proved to be instrumental in improving health and well-being when incorporated in your diet. The great part is that most of these ingredients are easily available and very simple to include in your everyday health and wellness regime, even when living the jet-set millennial life!

1. Ghee/*Ghrta*/Clarified Butter

In Ayurveda, ghee is called the 'carrier of nutrients'. It helps lubricate the intestinal tract and other organs in the body.

Ghee contains high amounts of vitamins A, D, E and K. These are fat-soluble vitamins, that is, vitamins that enter our bloodstream through the medium of fat. Ghee has lots of dietary fats that enable our body to absorb and make use of these vitamins. Including it regularly in your diet improves brain activity as well as general immunity.

One of the things that make ghee so good is the fact that it is mostly composed of saturated, 'good' fat, which promotes the increase of HDL or good cholesterol in the body. Being free of trans and hydrogenated fats makes it much easier to digest as compared to other types of fat. Having 1 teaspoon of ghee in the morning followed by warm water is said to regulate bowel movement.

According to Ayurveda, ghee mixed with honey can be applied on wounds, blisters and inflammation to effectively cure them. It is also applied to body joints to increase mobility. We've always known ghee is good—now the world knows it too!

2. Haldi/*Haridra*/Turmeric

From *haldi wala doodh* to Turmeric Latte, haldi has become the queen of every Ayurvedic kitchen and now even international coffee houses!

Loaded with antibacterial, antiviral and antifungal properties, turmeric is one of the best ingredients for your body. Whether you ingest it or apply it externally on your skin, it will only do you good! Haldi also helps improve blood circulation, which in turn lowers the density of bad cholesterol, chances of strokes, heart attacks, the formation of clots and heart problems.

Turmeric also heals wounds and injury scars by helping in the regeneration of damaged tissues and cells. These healing properties in haldi are attributed mainly to the presence of an antioxidant called curcumin which helps fight against all kinds of bacteria ranging from colds and viral infections to cuts and wounds, keeping your overall immunity at a steady high.

So the next time you are offered a glass or *haldi wala doodh*, make sure you gulp it down without pulling a face. Don't forget to add a pinch of pepper to it because 'pepperine' in the pepper helps the body absorb the curcumin from the turmeric much better.

3. Gwarphata/*Ghrit kumari*/Aloe Vera

Aloe vera falls under the bitter taste category in Ayurveda. This medicinal herb is cooling in nature and finds application in several digestive and dermatology-related ailments.

The aloe vera plant is called *Ghrita Kumari* in Sanskrit where *kumari* means a young girl, a very fitting name because of how useful this plant is in easing symptoms of menstruation and skin problems in women.

Aloe vera is also great when it comes to treating skin problems. Just applying natural gel from the plant is enough to nourish and hydrate your skin, get rid of irritation, sunburns, inflammation and signs of skin psoriasis caused because of dry skin. Even people with the most sensitive skin types find relief in aloe vera gel.

Besides applying it on your skin, you can also add it to your diet in small doses. A shot of aloe vera juice early in the morning is a great source of antioxidants that will work wonders for your immunity, digestion and skin.

4. Ashwagandha/Indian Ginseng

Ashwagandha in Sanskrit literally means 'smell of the horse'. It gets this name because of its unique smell and the ability to provide the strength of the stallion to its consumer.

One of the reasons why it is important to include this in today's jet-set lifestyle is because of its properties that aid in relieving stress and anxiety and combating depression. It also helps stabilize sleep patterns and reduce insomnia.

Ashwagandha is also commonly known as Indian ginseng, and preparations with honey and ghee work as an aphrodisiac. It is particularly helpful in treating fertility problems in men because it increases testosterone levels, libido and sperm count.

The leaves of Ashwagandha are known for their anti-inflammatory properties. They can be made into a paste and used for treating wounds and swellings.

You can consume Ashwagandha in the form of *churan*s, which are easily available online and in Ayurvedic stores across the country. You can also get them in a tablet form, like multivitamins.

5. Amla/*Amalaki*/Indian Gooseberry

Amla is another one of those Ayurvedic ingredients that help balance all the three *doshas—vata, pitta and kapha*. It can be eaten fresh as fruit or consumed in a powder or juice form.

It is great for weight loss. The high fibre and protein content in the fruit keeps you full for longer hours and controls cravings. It also helps check cholesterol levels.

Amla is also one of the best anti-ageing ingredients in Ayurveda. Amla juice mixed with honey and/or mashed papaya applied on the skin helps treat wrinkles and fine lines while acting as an exfoliator.

Starting your day with a little shot of Amla juice is a great way to ensure good eyesight, and glowing skin and hair.

6. Adrak/*Adraki*/Ginger

Ginger root is known as the 'universal medicine' in Ayurveda for its all-round benefits.

Living in urban times, with the constant temperature changes, pollution and lack of open spaces, makes one very easily susceptible to respiratory conditions, colds and allergies. Ayurveda promotes the use of ginger in many herbal decongestants and helps in minimizing these symptoms.

Ginger also has the ability to calm an upset stomach, promote the flow of bile, ease stomach cramps and improve the working of the digestive system. Mix grated ginger root with diluted lemon juice to soothe the digestive tract, reduce flatulence and treat stomach aches.

Regular massages with ginger oil can help relieve painful arthritis due to its anti-inflammatory properties.

7. Ajwain/*Yamani*/Carom Seeds

Ajwain is 'warm' in nature, helps balance *kapha* and *vata*, and increases *pitta dosha* or heat and metabolism in the body.

Ajwain is a commonly used spice in the Indian kitchen, but is also known to have medicinal properties in Ayurveda.

A teaspoon of ajwain and jaggery paste eaten once a day helps reduce the effects of asthma. Inhaling the smoke from roasting ajwain helps stabilize breathing, nasal congestion and relaxes the respiratory system.

Just chew on a pinch of roasted carom seeds to cure most problems related to the digestive tract—from flatulence to indigestion to acidity.

Crushed ajwain seeds and curd made into a paste and applied on the skin for a few minutes helps cure pimples and scars. It also helps avoid premature greying of hair.

8. Shahad/*Madhu*/Honey

Sweet and luscious, honey really is liquid gold. Its health benefits are countless—from providing relief from asthma, aiding digestion, relieving pain, treating burns to curing stomach ailments.

Begin your day with a glass of warm water with honey and lemon—it keeps you energetic, is a great detoxifying agent and also helps you trim your waistline.

Replacing sugar with honey is a very good idea at least in dishes where it is possible, like in your breakfast cereal, juices and smoothies. Slowly work your way into using it in desserts and *mithai*s too!

It is a natural humectant, which means that it adds moisture or humidity naturally, which makes it a great ingredient for dry skin.

> A face mask made of honey, some powdered oats, and cream or milk will give you soft, nourished, cleansed and moisturized skin within days of use.

After diving into the super foods that give our body the nourishment it needs and boosts your immune system, let's get into action by jotting down recipes by the chef. As you'd expect, this includes darn yummy low-calorie meals—recipes to make your skin glow and also enhance your vision. That's right, it's time to lose your glasses and use them as a fashion statement only when you wish to.

I. RECIPES FOR GLOWING SKIN

1. AMLA JUICE

It's amazing what this humble super food can do for your glow. Packed with Vitamin C, this fruit helps in cell renewal and replenishes the skin.

8 Indian gooseberries (*amla*)
2 inches ginger
4 teaspoons cumin seeds

- Combine Indian gooseberries, ginger and cumin seeds in a blender jar. Add 5 cups water and blend well.
- Strain and serve chilled.

2. CILANTRO AND SOYA STIR-FRIED BEAN SPROUTS

1 tablespoon chopped fresh cilantro leaves
2 teaspoons soy sauce
250 g bean sprouts
2 teaspoons unrefined oil
2 spring onion bulbs, diagonally sliced
1 medium carrot, cut into diagonal slices
¾ inch piece ginger, sliced
1 medium green capsicum, diced
Sea salt to taste
100 g bean curd, cut into cubes
2 spring onion green stalks, sliced

5–6 black peppercorns, crushed

- Heat oil in a pan. Add the spring onions, carrots and ginger and sauté for a minute.
- Add capsicum, bean sprouts, soy sauce, sea salt and stir for 2 minutes.
- Add bean curd, spring onion greens, coriander and crushed peppercorns and toss.
- Serve hot.

3. SPROUTS APPLE AND KIWI SALAD

1½ cups bean sprouts, blanched
2 apples
1 kiwi, peeled and cut into small pieces
6–8 iceberg lettuce leaves
1 medium onion, sliced
1 medium tomato, chopped

For dressing

2 tablespoons olive oil
¼ cup apple juice
1 tablespoon lemon juice
½ teaspoon black pepper powder
½ teaspoon mustard paste
Salt to taste

- Wash and soak the lettuce leaves in ice-cold water for about 15 minutes.

- To make the dressing, put the olive oil, lemon juice, apple juice, black pepper powder, mustard paste and salt in a small bowl and whisk well.
- Chop the apples into small pieces. Place them with the sprouts, onion and tomato in a large bowl.
- Drain the lettuce leaves, tear them into bite-sized pieces, and add them to the sprout mixture and toss.
- Add kiwi and mix with light hand.
- Pour the dressing on the salad and toss lightly. Serve immediately.

II. LOW-CALORIE RECIPES

1. BEET BERRY SMOOTHIE

1 small beetroot, peeled and cut in cubes
12–16 blackberries
5–6 strawberries + for garnishing
10–12 gooseberries
12–16 fresh blueberries
8–10 walnuts, roughly chopped
2 tablespoons tender coconut cream
16–20 fresh mint leaves
2 cups yogurt

- Blend together the blackberries, strawberries, gooseberries, beetroot, blueberries, walnuts, coconut cream, mint leaves and yogurt till smooth.
- Garnish individual tall glasses with strawberries, pour the smoothie in them and serve immediately.

2. SOYA GALOUTI

2 cups soya granules, soaked and squeezed
2 teaspoons ghee
1½ tablespoons ginger–garlic paste
3 tablespoons gram flour (*besan*)
1 teaspoon red chilli powder
1 teaspoon garam masala powder
½ teaspoon mace (*javitri*) powder
¼ teaspoon green cardamom (*elaichi*) powder
1 tablespoon browned onion paste
1 teaspoon screwpine (*kewra*) essence
Salt to taste
Few saffron strands (*kesar*), soaked in water

For garnishing

Chopped fresh coriander leaves
Curd onion rings
Lemon wedges

- Heat 1 teaspoon ghee in a non-stick pan. Add the ginger–garlic paste and sauté for 2–3 minutes.
- Add gram flour, mix and sauté till fragrant.
- Add the soya granules, mix and sauté for a minute.
- Add the chilli powder, garam masala powder, mace powder and cardamom powder, mix, and sauté for 4–5 minutes.
- Remove from heat and cool down to room temperature.

- Grind the soya mixture with browned onion paste and screwpine essence to a smooth paste.
- Transfer into a bowl, add salt and saffron along with the 1 tablespoon water, and mix well.
- Heat the remaining ghee in a non-stick pan.
- Dampen your palms, divide the mixture into equal portions and shape them into thin *tikki*s.
- Place the *tikki*s in the pan and shallow fry, flipping them occasionally till golden brown on both sides.
- Garnish with coriander leaves and serve hot with curd onion rings and lemon wedges.

3. VEGETABLE QUINOA PULAO

2 teaspoons ghee
1½ teaspoons caraway seeds (*shahi jeera*)
1 bay leaf
2–3 cloves
1-inch cinnamon
4–6 black peppercorns
1 star anise
1 medium onion, sliced
1½ cups quinoa, soaked for 1 hour
3 cups vegetable stock + as required
1 tablespoon chopped garlic
1 teaspoon red chilli powder
¼ teaspoon turmeric powder
8–10 cauliflower florets
1 medium carrot, peeled and cut into diamonds

5–6 French beans, diagonally sliced
3 tablespoons green peas
Salt to taste
1 tablespoon chopped fresh coriander leaves
Fresh coriander sprig for garnishing

- Heat 1 teaspoon ghee in a deep non-stick pan. Add 1 teaspoon caraway seeds, bay leaf, cloves, cinnamon, black peppercorns and star anise, mix, and sauté till fragrant.
- Add the onion and sauté till translucent.
- Add drained quinoa and mix.
- Add vegetable stock and salt, stir. Cover and cook till the quinoa is fully done.
- Heat remaining ghee in a non-stick pan. Add the remaining caraway seeds and garlic, mix, and sauté till the garlic turns golden brown.
- Add the chilli powder and turmeric powder and mix.
- Add the cauliflower, carrots and a little vegetable stock, mix, and cook for 2–3 minutes.
- Add French beans, green peas and add some more vegetable stock, mix and cook for a minute.
- Add salt and toss well.
- Add the cooked vegetables to the quinoa and mix well.
- Switch off heat, add coriander leaves and mix well.
- Serve hot, garnished with a coriander sprig.

4. PAPAYA SMOOTHIE BOWL

4 oranges
8 medium carrots, peeled
A few mint leaves
8 tablespoons pumpkin seeds
8 tablespoons honey
2 cups yogurt
A few ice cubes
2 small papayas, peeled, cut into 1-inch cubes and chilled
Fresh mint sprigs for garnish

- Peel the oranges, separate segments, remove the seeds and put them into a blender jar.
- Cut carrots into medium-sized pieces and add to the jar.
- Add mint leaves, pumpkin seeds, honey and yogurt, and blend into a smooth mixture.
- Add a few ice cubes and blend again.
- For serving, take the chilled papaya cubes in a bowl, and pour the smoothie over them.
- Garnish with mint sprigs and serve chilled.

Dr Barbara Sturm's Skincare Advice

How hectic is it going to a dermatologist?

First of all, a good one isn't easy on the pocket, but skin being the largest organ of your body, you just can't *not* prioritize it.

After consultation comes the tricky bit—many times it just doesn't work either, and it's hard to trust too many chemicals (especially steroids, the master ingredient in most medicines).

Puberty, pregnancy, early–mid–late twenties and menopause—basically your whole life is a hormonal roller coaster. These hormonal milestones define your skin health and you need different kinds of care for every stage.

How overwhelming, right? Is this ever going to stop? Will your skin ever be settled for a long time? No, there are going to be changes only to remind you that you are a beautiful woman going through life. But yes, if you have done the smart deed of picking up this book, you are in luck, as a top Hollywood dermatologist and scientist has decided to drop some knowledge here.

Excited? How excited will you be if I tell you this top Hollywood dermat treats Kim Kardashian, Bella Hadid, Kate Moss, Rosie Huntington-Whiteley, Gwyneth Paltrow, Hailey Baldwin Bieber, Cher . . . the list goes on—but you get the point.

It was a proud moment for me to interview Dr Barbara Sturm, a gorgeous German dermat and scientist who makes the biggest celebrities on earth radiate. Not just that, her carefully formulated skincare line balances skin so well that it's a 'must-have' in almost every celebrity's travel bag.

1. At what age should millennials plan to use anti-ageing products?

Starting from a young age, you should follow an anti-inflammatory skincare regime. Your skincare products shouldn't contain harmful ingredients such as mineral oils. As you get older, puberty and hormones kick in, so you shouldn't be using products that are too harsh on your skin, or products that dry out your skin. If you aren't taking care of your skin or are using the wrong products, sebum production will become unbalanced and your skin barrier function won't perform as well. When your skin is dry, it starts to have little injuries, and bacteria could start settling in, causing more breakouts. It is therefore really important to keep your skin hydrated and healthy with a very simple anti-inflammatory skincare routine. If you choose to use anti-ageing products, you should use regenerative ingredients which are directed towards healing and anti-inflammation, such as purslane. Anti-oxidants and peptides won't hurt either, but you should also watch your lifestyle choices, as this can have a big impact on your ageing.

2. What is the most common skincare myth?

The most common skincare myth is to drink water instead of using a skincare regime and that drinking water will also stop your skin from ageing. Another common myth is that 'more is more'. I always believe that 'less is more'. It is really important not to overpower your skin with lots of different products, especially at a young age. I recommend using a gentle cleanser, a facial scrub and a quality cream to rejuvenate your skin. If you tend to have dry skin, use a hydrating face mask and hyaluronic serum to keep you looking refreshed and radiant.

3. The most common beauty advice people wrongly give.

I believe the worst common beauty advice is to use aggressive treatments like acid peels or laser resurfacing, as these treatments can harm your skin.

4. How often and how should one cleanse the skin? (I read in one of your interviews that we should be washing our face less, hence very curious.)

A good cleansing routine is very important and shouldn't dry out your skin. Our bestselling cleanser, for example, uses aloe vera and urea among its active ingredients. It's a foaming cleanser that hydrates.

It's really important that you don't use facial wipes to remove makeup or to cleanse your face because these can hurt your skin and rub dirt and bacteria into your skin further. I recommend using a very gentle cleanser and only double cleanse if you are wearing heavy makeup, as over-cleansing disturbs the skin barrier function and balance.

You should also exfoliate twice a week. Exfoliation is important because if you don't get rid of your dead skin cells, active ingredients can't come through, leaving your skin dehydrated. Another important factor to consider is that skin cells together with the oil from sebum production oxygenate and can cause blackheads and breakouts.

5. The one overly popular/over-hyped ingredient that's actually not all that great.

I would stay away from using glycolic and retinol acids because these can destroy skin barrier function by removing healthy layers of skin, which can cause inflammation, making your skin worse. Glycolic and retinol acids can also cause hyperpigmentation issues, ageing, premature ageing and possibly cancer.

6. Worst foods and beverages for skin we should be avoiding.

This one you should know! We should be avoiding processed meat, sodas, fried food and alcohol where possible.

7. What would be the most common skin concern you've treated in your many years of practice and what's rule #1 to treat it?

I think the most common skin concern is dryness, because dryness can cause breakouts and ageing. I therefore believe it's important to keep our skin hydrated, which led me to create Dr Barbara Sturm Hyaluronic Serum. This is a must-have in your skincare routine, and the highly concentrated long and short-chain hyaluronic molecules provide intensive hydration. It's not about being oily or greasy—it's all about hydration.

8. Acne, pigmentation, blemishes—can you list one fool-proof way each to treat these problems.

My one fool-proof way to treat acne, pigmentation and blemishes is to keep your face hydrated. Live a healthy lifestyle, adopt an anti-inflammatory skincare routine and avoid using acid peels, full stop.

9. Everyone knows fast food is bad for skin, but if you have to come up with a junk food eater's beauty regime what would that be?

Don't eat junk food!

10. What have millennials got wrong about beauty? (about the concept of beauty, the lifestyle pattern or experimentation by giving into too many options.)

I think millennials are quite smart in their skincare routine. They want to know exactly what ingredients are in the products they are using and are interested in what works and what doesn't work for their skin. I feel millennials don't just go for marketing promises. They actually dig deeper and have a better and clearer understanding about what their skin can tolerate and what their skin needs.

11. Best way for a busy girl to have good skin?

The best way for a busy girl to have good skin is to always remember that less is more. It's also important to have a good cleanser, hyaluronic serum and a good cream—that's all you need!

12. What do you have to say about changing beauty trends? Like jade rollers, etc.? How much importance should we be giving to every new trend that we see on the Internet?

Jade facial rollers are cool. Not only do they massage your skin, but they also boost blood circulation and actually trigger your skin to promote your fibroplasia skin cells, enhancing collagen production. I think those treatments are great.

Master Perfumer Roja Dove

On finding your signature scent:

Scents are so personal. Sometimes you may buy it casually, but it's only over time that you realize that some of those purchases don't really belong to you. Often what's the case is that the same perfume you loved so much on someone you met at a party didn't translate so well on you . . . which makes you buy a few more just to add that right bout of floral, fruity, woody, classic, or musky twist that you can't pin down but will recognize immediately when you smell it again.

Fragrances are considered one of the strongest memories. Just a spray can bring back a thousand memories. A city you always wanted to return to, a special someone who hasn't crossed your mind for a while, or a faint memory from childhood—perfumes can have sentimental value without you even being aware of it.

But what beginners (and many perfume lovers) struggle with is finding a scent that defines them. Have you heard people boasting of sticking with one perfume for decades? That's not strictly out of liking or loyalty—they wear it because it is their signature scent.

Day or night, weekend or weekday, there's a scent for everyone that they can wear and give people around them a memory to remember them by.

While you might buy fragrances that smelled like a piece of heaven in the store, if they don't quite define your personality there's no ownership and it just doesn't feel right.

In relationship terms, it can be like being married to an incompatible person. But worry not, you don't have to go through all that to meet your soulmate . . . sorry, I meant perfume.

Being a big-time connoisseur myself, I've helped a lot of friends discover their signature scents, but for the reader of *Roots to Radiance* I settled for nothing but the best and paved the path for the finest perfumers in the business to help you figure out the dos and don'ts of perfume shopping.

Roja Dove, a British perfumer born in Sussex, is one of the finest noses and fragrance historians that ever lived. Dove started chasing perfumes quite early in the day. He was amazed to find how small perfume bottles could store something so effective. His interest in perfumes sparked when his mother's fragrance lingered in his room long after she put him to bed and kissed him goodnight, and little did he know that he would one day be the most sought-after perfume expert that ever lived. After serving a big French fragrance label, Roja now makes his own luxury perfumes that sell worldwide.

And in the middle of all the creative formulation, he has taken out the time to help you decide a fragrance that'll not just become a part of your identity, but for most people you meet it may just become synonymous with your memory. So, take notes:

1. Go it alone. Never take a friend along while making a choice this personal. You have your perfume agenda—they have one that's completely different. Something you love on yourself, they may think doesn't suit you at all. Contrary to what you may currently believe, it has little to do with how perfume develops on the skin. The idea that fragrances smell different on each individual is becoming a thing of the past. The more synthetics are used in the creation process, the less individual the fragrance will smell. A fragrance has to suit a wearer's personality.

2. Try lots! But how many can you try in one shopping day? More than you imagine if you take time. If you smell fragrances freshly sprayed, your nose will tire after the third one or so. This is due to the alcohol content,

which works like an anaesthetic. It's a bit like drinking three gin and tonics and still expecting to have razor-sharp perception.

Smelling the perfume on paper on the 'dry down' (when the perfume has settled and the alcohol has evaporated) means you can smell fragrances all day without fatigue. Testing on paper is the only sane way to try a fragrance. It's free from glues or binders and is as near to skin as is possible to recreate. The only thing missing is the warmth of the skin, so breathe out very hard on them to warm them up before you inhale.

Spray a few on blotter cards, turn them over to conceal the brand and then smell them away from the perfumery department. Maybe take yourself to a smart little bar and slowly sniff and deliberate alongside a glass of well-chilled champagne. After all, this could become a long-term love affair and it needs to be approached like a game of seduction—slowly and with pleasure.

Smell them one at a time, comparing each one to the next, eliminating the one you like least of the two you're comparing, then continue the process until you have only one or a maximum of two left, then turn the card to see which one has seduced you.

3. Always have unperfumed skin when going to buy a new scent, or the scents will fight against each other.

Now go back to the counter and spray one and only one on your skin. And it shouldn't be a small squirt on your wrist. Spray it all over, then go away and sleep on it. A quick sniff is like flirting —just like a lover. It's only when you spend the night together that you know if the relationship is going to work out or not.

If you're still in love in the morning, then buy it.

Now, before you head out to meet your soulmate, you are lucky that this relationship expert aka perfumer has also given you cues to help you choose better.

Here is Roja's elaboration on prominent ingredients in the olfaction family:

1. Amber

A hugely popular note in perfumery is amber, which is interesting, as amber does not exist in perfumery per se. It is a term that causes huge confusion, as many people use it without understanding its meaning. It has nothing to do with the fossilized resin used in jewellery and is generally used to describe synthetic ambergris. It is often used to describe oriental harmonies, created from a blend of benzoin, labdanum and vanilla. True ambergris, when used, is a completely ecological material as it is a natural secretion from the sperm whale, but because it is so rare, and so exquisitely beautiful in its odour, it is one of the most-cherished and least-used materials in the perfumers canon.

2. Aoud

Agarwood, also known as aoud, oud, or oudh, is the resinous heartwood of the aquilaria tree. The heartwood becomes diseased, leaving it dark, oily and incredibly dense. The wood becomes so dense that it does not float. The oil is distilled from the wood and the wood is still burnt in the traditional manner, known as *bakhoor*, making it one of the oldest forms of incense in the world. It is a relative of sandalwood and has been used for longer than any other material we know of. It has an incredible depth and it sits very low down in the composition of a fragrance, meaning it lasts and lasts on the skin. It has the ability to hold other materials in place, making it an excellent fixative. Like all materials, it varies hugely in quality as many aouds on the market are of poor quality, and/or have very little aoud in them.

It is still the scent of choice in the Middle East and is now formally established in Western perfumery. It was Tom Ford who brought this fashion to the West when he launched Oud Wood in 2008, adding touches of it to Noir et Noir and Tuscan Leather in the same year. His Private Blends were so influential that other perfumers quickly followed suit in the same year, showing the breadth of interest and diversity of houses who wanted to capture a little of the glamour and exoticism that aoud imparts.

3. Bergamot

It is no grand statement to make when one says that citrus notes are found in more or less all perfumery creations. They create a pleasurable introduction to the fragrance, giving it vitality and freshness. These notes dissipate quicker than any other materials, which is why a perfume 'evolves' over time—these citrus notes help to make a perfume less heavy at its starting point. You can use lemon or lime or grapefruit, for example, but of all the citrus notes, there is no other quite like bergamot. It is the finest of the citrus notes and is obtained from the fruit of Citrus *bergamia*, which grows throughout Southern Italy—the best coming from Calabria. The finest quality is still obtained by pressing the oil from the rind by hand on to a sea sponge. This is extremely labour-intensive and is basically no longer done. It takes 1500 kg of bergamot to produce 1 kg of oil. Like all hesperidic fruits, the oil is very volatile and therefore doesn't last long. Whilst it is still very fresh, it is much richer and more rounded than any of the other citrus notes which smell somewhat one-dimensional in comparison, making bergamot a highly prized ingredient.

4. Rose

Man has been fascinated with rose since the time of the ancient Egyptians, who used it amongst other things for medical purposes. Homer and Sappho also refer to it, but it was the Middle Eastern perfumers who perfected the commercial distillation of rose water around the seventh or eighth century. There are various types of rose available to the perfumer—each one has its own specific olfactory quality. They each add a cool serenity to a composition and are often used to temper the overt sensuality of white blossoms.

Growing mainly in Grasse, *Rose de Mai* is like kryptonite for the perfumer. It produces the finest-quality oil on earth, displaying a honeyed odour underscored by a warm, peppery note. Not only is it the finest quality, but it is also one of the most notoriously difficult floral perfumery materials to harvest as it flowers only in the month of May (hence its name).

It takes over 3,00,000 roses picked before the sun gains strength in the morning to produce just 1 kg of oil. After the sun comes up, the amount of oil within the rose diminishes, and by noon it would require a further 50 per cent of blossoms to produce the same yield of oil—so it is better to wait until the next day.

It is essential to understand that this process is very labour-intensive as there is no mechanization involved. It costs tens of thousands of euros per kilo to produce, so it is literally worth its weight in gold.

Very few perfumers will use Rose de Mai in their fragrances, settling instead for the cheaper Bulgarian rose.

Rose is used in majority of all perfume compositions. Many are surprised to see just how many male scents it is used in, but when you consider the fact that a rose on a man will smell masculine and a rose on a woman will smell feminine, it starts to make sense. The rose has no masculine or feminine leanings—it is how the flower is dressed up in a fragrance accord that determines its 'gender'.

5. Sandalwood

The finest sandalwood essential oil is obtained from *Santalum album*, which comes from Mysore in India. The tree needs to be a minimum of 30 years old before it displays its typical sweet, warm and smooth odour, so its harvesting is strictly regulated by the government. It is an extremely difficult material to balance in a creation, as it plays tricks with one's sense of smell—one moment it is there and then the next it disappears.

Sandalwood is legendary for the lingering quality it brings to a perfume. It is one of the most expensive of all perfume raw materials and has also been used for longer than most.

It comes as no surprise then that sandalwood is used so commonly in perfumery—it is like a trigger word to many people. It is nothing if not beautiful, and to use it (well) in a composition is a sure-fire way for a perfumer's creation to be loved.

6. Vanilla

Vanilla absolute is obtained from the seed pod of the tropical orchid *Vanilla planifolia*, which is grown commercially in Madagascar and Réunion as a result of the French creating plantations in the nineteenth century. Fine-grade vanilla will take 18 months of treatment before it will be used in perfumery. The finest quality, *Vanilla Bourbon*, takes roughly 24 months to produce. It is an excellent fixative and is indispensable for the creation of oriental harmonies.

Vanilla is a psychogenic aphrodisiac, enhancing all sensations of pleasure, and is one of the most expensive of all spices, so there is no wonder why it is used so regularly across perfumery. We as humans have a positive biological response to it, and its warm, soft and balsamic odour really helps to make a perfume well-rounded. However, vanilla can often be substituted for *Vanillin* in cheaper creations, which just doesn't have the same effect.

7. Vetiver

Vetiver essential oil is obtained from the root of an Indian grass, *Vetiveria zizanioides*, which grows nearly 2 metres in height. It is an exceptionally fine and important fixative. Today, the main producers are Indonesia, Haiti and Réunion, with the finest coming from the latter. Whilst it is considered a masculine note, it is used in nearly 40 per cent of all feminine compositions, providing a backbone on which to work the other materials. Its scent is so warm, it smells dry—conveying earthy, leathery and smoky aspects.

Shrankhla Holecek: Uma Oils

The world is moving towards finding holistic solutions to every problem. While the healing process is very different from non-Ayurvedic methods, many of these organic solutions can end most of our concerns for good. We all hate popping pills because of the damages it could do to our body. But no one said you can't address a concern without having to worry about the side effects.

This chapter of *Roots to Radiance* features a very special beauty entrepreneur—Shrankhla Holecek, founder of Uma Oils—who's advocating the pros of holistic beauty all over the world. Going by how stressed millennials were back then (which we still are in current times), she quit her management job and turned to her roots to seek answers for lifelong wellness and beauty. Her brand may be a collection of most uniquely formulated luxurious oils, but it didn't happen out of the blue.

She hails from a family of generational veterans who have mastered the craft of organic essential oil production and have supplied some of the world's leading luxury beauty brands for decades. But the question is, where are these luxurious oils made?

Most definitely in India (Raipur) and roughly 30 kilometres from where I grew up.

Yes, I spent most of my life not knowing that the biggest beauty brands in the world are using the oils extracted out of an estate so close to my home. I came to know all about them only after they blew up the 'gram with their amazingly packaged and philosophically strong products.

Small world, right? If that wasn't enough, to my surprise, I came to know that we shared the same second name until she got married. But meeting another Upadhyay of Chhattisgarh wasn't the factor that made me reach out to her—it was the unique ways her brand treats several disorders with essential oils. And no, it isn't by skin type and other basic approaches. This thing goes deep within. They segregate disorders and classify them into three biological energies, aka, *doshas*—*vata*, *pitta* and *kapha*.

According to their philosophy, identifying your dosha is crucial, as it is your individual constitution. Treating your body according to it will lead you to achieve balance.

There are three states of the three doshas: balanced, increased and decreased.

Balanced means the doshas are present in their ideal proportions, which is also known as achieving the state of equilibrium.

Increased refers to beyond the normal proportion, also referred to as an 'aggravated' state.

Decreased: This is the depleted state, where you're deprived of certain qualities, making you fall out of balance.

Here's how it's made simpler:

Dosha	In Balance	Out of Balance
Vata (Qualities affecting the elements of Space and Air)	High energy, creative, friendly	Dry skin/hair, anxiety, spacey
Pitta (Qualities affecting the elements of Fire and Water)	Strength, courage, proper digestion, boost in confidence	Aggression, insomnia, inflammation
Kapha (Qualities affecting the elements of Water and Earth)	Loyalty, calmness, generosity	Depression, discontentment, stubbornness

For this chapter, I pinned down this natural medicine practitioner to throw some light on essential oil blends, easing beauty struggles and more.

1. Essential Oil Pairings

Anti-ageing: Frankincense Oil + Juniper Berry Oil
Calming sensitivity: Chamomile Oil + Lavender Oil
Blemishes: Tea Tree Oil + Clove Oil
Hyperpigmentation: Ylang Ylang Oil + Orange Oil
Simple everyday scent: Sandalwood Oil + Jasmine Oil

2. Flowers, herbs, clays and leaves—top favourite ingredients for healthy skin and hair

Scalp nourishment: Hibiscus flowers
Brightening and glow: Saffron flowers
Pore cleaning and cleansing: Bentonite clay
Depigmentation: Fenugreek leaves
Hair growth: Curry leaves
Battling blemishes: Mint leaves

3. Body and face toning homemade mask: Banana and sandalwood with gram flour (alternatively: gram flour or oatmeal).

Loaded with Vitamin B6, and a good source of iron, manganese, Vitamin C, potassium, biotin and copper, bananas are excellent for the skin. This easy-to-prepare mask works best when applied once in two weeks.

- Take a ripe banana and mash it until it reaches an even consistency.

- Mix in sandalwood powder (or oatmeal or gram flour), and apply it all over the face and neck.
- Allow the mask to dry for 10 minutes before rinsing off.

The nutrients in banana rejuvenate the skin, retard the ageing process and prevent the appearance of wrinkles. Sandalwood helps balance skin's oil production (helping both dry and oily skin's alike, as it moderates oil production as opposed to adding or taking away oil to the face). Sandalwood also calms inflammations and gives the skin a radiant glow.

4. Homemade dark spot correcting mask: Carrots with honey and lemon

- Mash a medium-sized carrot to a pulp in your food processor (alternatively you can grate it).
- Add 2 tablespoons of organic honey and 1 teaspoon of fresh lemon juice to this mix (skip the lemon juice if your skin is sensitive to it).
- Apply this mixture to cleansed skin and leave on for 20–30 minutes before rinsing off with lukewarm water.

Carrots are a rich source of beta-carotene and vitamins C and K, ingredients that are beneficial for the skin as they slow down the ageing process and deeply moisturize the skin. Lemon lightens dark spots and aids in cellular turnover, and honey is an excellent natural antibacterial agent. Together, this is a super-ingredient mask that works for every skin type!

5. DIY Depigmenting Mask: Almond flour with milk powder, honey and rose water

This is a potent DIY face mask for those bothered by dry skin and skin blemishes!

- Mix 2 tablespoons each of milk powder and almond flour (available more readily than you'd imagine at your local grocer!) with 1 tablespoon each of honey and rose water.
- Apply this paste evenly to the face and neck region, allowing it about 20 minutes to dry.
- Rinse with cold water.

Almond flour, milk and honey deeply nourish the skin, while rose water serves as a toner. This mask can be applied daily and is extremely helpful in lightening blemishes. In case of spot pigmentation problems, apply the mask and leave on overnight.

Acknowledgements

I was told writing a book is one of the hardest things I'll ever do and that it's as painful as giving birth. I don't agree with any of that *at all*.

As far as giving birth is concerned, it is also considered one of the most fulfilling things women can do. I know nothing about that (yet), but writing this book definitely is the most fulfilling act I've ever done.

The majority of this book has been written at midnight, but boy, have I found that to be the best time to work! Through this book I've realized that I'm not only *not* a morning person, but also that I'm a pretty good midnight person when it comes to writing and productivity.

Living alone and having a full-time job, among other stuff, didn't leave a lot of choice for me to pick a better time to do this, but I'll tell you what—when the clock strikes midnight the only things we worry about are the things we really love and care about. And that forms a beautiful link to work its way into a project you're investing in.

For me this isn't just another project; to me this book is #LOVE in 288 pages. It's the magic, chaos, happenings and instances from everyday life channelled into words you may relate with.

Apart from thanking my dad, mom, brother, grandmother and three cousins back home for motivating me in the process, special thanks go to Mr P for constantly pushing me and motivating me to dream and achieve bigger.

To my oldest friends, Joice Cherian and Mahima Jain, for being the first ones besides immediate family to shape my self-esteem so well since childhood. Look at what you've done, you two!

To all the contributors in this book, my mother Sushma Upadhyay, Dia Mirza, Bobbi Brown, Sanjeev Kapoor, Dr Barbara Sturm, Shrankhla Holecek, Roja Dove, and my editor, Swati Chopra, who gave me all the creative freedom I needed and welcomed all my ideas I had for this book, and also dragged me back to the right path whenever it needed to be done.

Not to miss Mriga Maithel and Bidisha Srivastava at Penguin Random House who helped edit the book and Devangana Dash who designed the fabulous cover.

I would like to thank Alyona Kapoor, Traccy Miichael, Esha Makwana, Sonica Sunderram, Jack Hewitt and Belinda Arnold—you know what you've done for this book, and I'm super grateful to you. Last but not the least, Ashish Sahu who clicked my author photo that fit right into the theme of the cover.

To all the bitter and sweet experiences in my life that have led me to being the person I like so much.

To everyone (good and bad) I've ever known—you always play your part perfectly.

About the Author

Nikita Upadhyay is the former digital head of Cosmopolitan, a website she grew organically from 9 million to 80 million in two years. She now does the same for renowned international brands worldwide. She is a beauty influencer and content creator online, and has worked with major cosmetic and wellness brands, including The Body Shop, Bath & Body Works, MAC, Kama Ayurveda, Innisfree to name a few, with major tie-ups with Amazon, Nykaa and other international luxury brands.

She has also practised Bharatnatyam for nine years and has performed at the national level. Apart from beauty, she also writes about travel and relationships on her website www.nikitaupadhyay.com and would love to see anything you create from this book on instagram: @nikitaupadhyay